T. E. LAWRENCE

LIVES OF NOTABLE GAY MEN AND LESBIANS

T. E. LAWRENCE

DANIEL WOLFE

MARTIN DUBERMAN, General Editor

CHELSEA HOUSE PUBLISHERS New York • Philadelphia

This book owes much to the work of Jan Morris, the brilliant transsexual historian. Like Lawrence, Morris was an Oxford man whose journey East helped him not only to write about the rulers of the Muslim holy places but to explore himself. Morris's writing—whether about Oxford, Arabia, or the British Empire—has been a crucial source of information, and an inspiring reminder of the power of transformation through travel.

First Printing

1 3 5 7 9 8 6 4 2

Library of Congress Cataloging-in-Publication Data

Wolfe, Daniel.
T. E. Lawrence/Daniel Wolfe.
p. cm.—(Lives of notable gay men and lesbians)
Includes bibliographical references (p.) and index.
ISBN 0-7910-2324-9
0-7910-2891-7 (pbk.)
1. Lawrence, T. E. (Thomas Edward), 1888–1935. 2. Great Britain. Army—Biography. 3. Soldiers—Great Britain—Biography. 4. World War, 1914–1918—Campaigns—Middle East. 5. Middle East—History, Military. 6. Gay men—Biography. I. Title. II. Series.
D568.4.L45W65 1995 94-27034
940.4'15'092—dc20 CIP
[B] AC

CONTENTS

Titles in

LIVES OF NOTABLE GAY MEN AND LESBIANS

ALVIN AILEY

JAMES BALDWIN

WILLA CATHER

JAMES DEAN

SERGEI DIAGHILEV

MARLENE DIETRICH

E. M. FORSTER

FEDERICO GARCÍA LORCA

ALLEN GINSBERG

LORRAINE HANSBERRY

J. EDGAR HOOVER

ROCK HUDSON

ELTON JOHN

JOHN MAYNARD KEYNES

K. D. LANG

T. E. LAWRENCE

LIBERACE

AUDRE LORDE

MARTINA NAVRATILOVA

GEORGIA O'KEEFFE

ADRIENNE RICH

BAYARD RUSTIN

SAPPHO

BESSIE SMITH

GERTRUDE STEIN

ALAN TURING

ANDY WARHOL

WALT WHITMAN

OSCAR WILDE

TENNESSEE WILLIAMS

VIRGINIA WOOLF

GAY, STRAIGHT, AND IN BETWEEN

by Martin Duberman

Being different is never easy. Especially in a culture like ours, which puts a premium on conformity and equates difference with deficiency. And especially during the teenage years when one feels desperate for acceptance and vulnerable to judgment. If you are taller or shorter than average, or fatter or thinner, or physically challenged, or of the "wrong" color, gender, religion, nationality, or sexual orientation, you are likely to be treated as "less than," as inferior to what the majority has decreed is the optimal, standard model.

Theoretically, those of us who are different should be delighted that we are *not* ordinary, not just another cookie-cutter product of mainstream culture. We should glory in the knowledge that many remarkably creative figures, past and present, lived outside accepted norms and pressed hard against accepted boundaries.

But in reality many of us have internalized the majority's standards of worth, and we do not feel very good about ourselves. How could we? When we look around us, we see that most people in high places of visibility, privilege, and power are white, heterosexual males of a very traditional kind. That remains true even though intolerance may have ebbed *somewhat* in recent decades and people of diverse backgrounds may have *begun* to attain more of a foothold in our culture.

Many gay men and lesbians through time have looked and acted like "ordinary" people and could therefore choose to "stay in the closet" and avoid social condemnation—though the effort at concealment produced its own turmoil and usually came at the price of self-acceptance. On the other hand, "sissy" gay men or "butch" lesbians have been quickly categorized and scorned by the mainstream culture as "sexual deviants"—even though no necessary link exists between gender nonconformity and sexual orientation. In the last 15 years or so, however, more and more people who previously would have passed as straight *have* been choosing to "come out." They sense that social consequences are no longer as severe as they once were—and that the psychic costs of concealment are taking too great a toll.

Yet even today, there are comparatively few role models available for gays and lesbians to emulate. And unlike other oppressed minorities, homosexuals don't often find confirmation within their own families. Even when a homosexual child is not rejected outright, acceptance comes within a family unit that is structurally heterosexual and in which homosexuality is generally mocked and decried. With his or her different desire and experience, the gay son or lesbian daughter remains an exotic. Moreover, such children are unable to find in family lore and traditions—as other minority people can—a compensatory source of validation to counterbalance the ridicule of mainstream culture.

Things are rarely any better at school, where textbooks and lessons are usually devoid of relevant information about homosexuality. Nor does the mainstream culture—movies or television, for example—often provide gays or lesbians with positive images of themselves, let alone any sense of historical antecedents. These silences are in large measure a reflection of the culture's homophobia. But to a lesser degree they reflect two other matters as well: the fact that many accomplished gay men and lesbians in the past refused to publicly acknowledge their sexuality (sometimes even to themselves); and secondly, the problem of assigning "gay" or "lesbian" identities to past figures who lived at a time when those conceptual categories did not exist.

For the surprising finding of recent scholarship is that categorizing human beings on the basis of sexual desire alone is a relatively recent phenomenon of the last several hundred years. It is a development, many historians believe, tied to the increasing urbanization of Europe and the Americas, and to the new opportunities city life presented for anonymity—for freedom from the relentless scrutiny of family and neighbors that had characterized farming communities and small towns. Only with the new freedom afforded by city life, historians are telling us, could people who felt they were different give free rein to their natures, lay claim to a distinctive identity, and begin to elaborate a subculture that would reflect it.

Prior to, say, 1700 (the precise date is under debate), the descriptive categories of "straight" or "gay" were not widely employed in dividing up human nature. Even today, in many non-Western parts of the world, it is unusual to categorize people on the basis of sexual orientation alone. Through time and across cultures it has often been assumed that *both* same- and opposite-gender erotic feelings (what we now call "bisexuality") could coexist in an individual—even if *acting* on same-gender impulses was usually taboo.

In the West, where we *do* currently divide humanity into oppositional categories of "gay" and "straight," most people grow up accepting that division as "natural" and dutifully assign themselves to one category or the other. Those who adopt the definition "gay" or "lesbian," however, soon discover that mainstream culture offers homosexuals (unlike heterosexuals) no history or sense of forebears. This is a terrible burden, especially during the teenage years, when one is actively searching for a usable identity, for a continuum in which to place oneself and lay claim to a contented and productive life.

This series is designed, above all, to fill that huge, painful cultural gap. It is designed to instill not only pride in antecedents but encouragement, the kind of encouragement that literature and biography have always provided: proof that someone else out there has felt what we have felt, experienced what we have experienced, been where we have been—and has endured, achieved, and flourished.

But *who* to include in this series has been problematic. Even today, many people refuse to define themselves as gay or lesbian. In some cases, they do not wish to confine what they view as their fluid sexuality into narrow, either/or categories. In other cases, they may acknowledge to themselves that their sexuality does fit squarely within the "gay" category, yet refuse to say so publicly, unwilling to take on the onus of a lesbian or gay identity. In still other cases, an individual's sense of sexual identity can change during his or her lifetime, as can his or her sense of its importance, when compared with many other strands, in defining their overall temperament.

Complicating matters still further is the fact that even today—when multitudes openly call themselves gay or lesbian, and when society as a whole argues about gay marriage and parenting or the place of gay people in the military—there is still no agreed-upon definition of what centrally constitutes a gay or lesbian identity. Should we call someone gay if his or her sexual desire is *predominantly* directed toward people of their own gender? But then how do we establish predominance? And by "desire" do we mean actual behavior—or fantasies that are never acted out? (Thus Father John McNeill, the writer and Jesuit, has insisted—though he has never actually had sex with another man—that on the basis of his erotic fantasies, he *is* a gay man.)

Some scholars and theorists even argue that genital sexuality need not be present in a relationship before we can legitimately call it gay or lesbian, stressing instead the central importance of same-gender *emotional* commitment. The problem of definition is then further complicated when we include the element of *self*-definition. If we come across someone in the past who does not explicitly self-identify as gay, by what right, and according to what evidence, can we claim them anyway?

Should we eliminate all historical figures who lived before "gay" or "lesbian" were available categories for understanding and ordering their experience? Are we entitled, for the purposes of this series, to include at least some of those from the past whose sexuality seems not to have been confined to one gender or the other, or who—as a cover, to protect a public image or a career—may have married, and thus have been commonly taken to be heterosexual? And if we do not include some of those whose sexuality cannot be clearly categorized as "gay," then how can we speak of a gay and lesbian continuum, a *history*?

In deciding which individuals to include in *Notable Gay Men and Lesbians,* I have gone back and forth between these competing definitions, juggling, combining, and, occasionally, finessing them. For the most part, I have tried to confine my choices to those figures who *by any definition* (same-gender emotional commitment, erotic fantasy, sexual behavior, *and* self-definition) do clearly qualify for inclusion.

But alas, we often lack the needed intimate evidence for such clear-cut judgments. I have regretfully omitted from the series many bisexual figures, and especially the many well-known women—Tallulah Bankhead, Judy Garland, Greta Garbo, or Josephine Baker, for example—whose erotic and emotional preference seem indeterminable (usually for lack of documentation). But I will probably also include a few—Margaret Mead, say, or Marlene Dietrich—as witnesses to the difficult ambiguities of sexual definition, and to allow for a discussion of those ambiguities.

In any case, I suspect much of the likely criticism over this or that choice will come from those eager to conceal their distaste for a series devoted to "Notable (no less!) Gay Men and Lesbians" under the guise of protesting a single inclusion or omission within it. That kind of criticism can be easily borne, and is more than compensated for, by the satisfaction of acquainting today's young gays and lesbians—and indeed all who feel "different"—with knowledge of some of those distinguished forebears whose existence can inform and comfort them.

T. E. Lawrence—known around the world as "Lawrence of Arabia"—is a deeply enigmatic figure. He was one of the most celebrated heroes of World War I, the blue-eyed Englishman who was (in the West, anyway) renowned as the "uncrowned king of the Arabs," yet his personal life gives the notion of secrecy a whole new dimension. And trying to peer behind the veils within veils of Lawrence's private world has proven a recipe for frustration—or invention—for several generations of biographers.

Only the most scrupulous of biographers (of Lawrence or of anyone) can resist the temptation to project their own fantasies onto the many blank pages in the record. In his frankness about Lawrence's personal life, as in his willingness to acknowledge the difficulty of separating fact from fiction, Daniel Wolfe is an ideal biographer for T. E. Lawrence. His success in portraying Lawrence, the man, is due first of all to his uncommon skills as a writer and as a careful sifter of evidence. But it is also due to Wolfe's willingness, as a gay man himself, to talk plainly about aspects of the extant evidence that previous biographers of Lawrence have skirted or misinterpreted.

The man Wolfe presents to us is first and foremost a puritan in temperament. As an undergraduate, Lawrence swam outdoors in midwinter, never drank, and seems rarely to have eaten. Aiming at self-mastery, he scorned indulgence of any kind. That is, except for perhaps the most dangerous of all indulgences: falling in love.

In Syria in 1911, Lawrence met the beautiful, fifteen-year-old Salim Ahmed—and was inseparable from him for the next four years. As Wolfe reminds us, it is still not uncommon in much of the Arab world for an older man to have sex with a teenage boy (and still more common, apparently, for unmarried young men to have sex with each other), so long as the older man plays the active (inserter) role in anal intercourse—and so long as the relationship is not spoken of publicly. The Western concept of a "gay man" makes little sense in an Arab world where every man is thought susceptible to the charms of an adolescent boy.

Lawrence later said that he had helped launch the Arabs' revolt against their Turkish rulers because he had "liked a particular Arab very much, and thought that freedom for his race would be an acceptable present." That may well have been romantic hyperbole. And so, too, may be the singularly important role in the Arab Revolt which Lawrence (and some of his admirers) would later claim for him. Unlike many of Lawrence's Western biographers, Arabs generally tend to characterize him as the "servant," not the leader of Feisal, Auda, and Hussein in helping to end Bedouin factionalism and to forge a unified, successful effort to throw off the yoke of Turkish domination. Helping the Arabs drive out the Turks, moreover, was clearly to British advantage: it would give them a leg up on the other colonial powers in the competition to dominate the Middle East. Lawrence—true friend of the Arabs though he was—was nonetheless steeped in the imperialist ethos that infected British policy in these years.

Wolfe tells the dramatic tale of the Arab Revolt, and Lawrence's role in it, with compelling verve. And he is no less compelling when recounting the transformation these adventures wrought in Lawrence himself. This is nowhere more apparent than in Wolfe's handling of the famous episode Lawrence described in his book *Seven Pillars of Wisdom,* in which he was supposedly beaten and raped by the Turkish official Hajim Bey. In recounting the inconsistencies and uncertainties of Lawrence's account, Wolfe emphasizes the primary importance of the story as a key to Lawrence's fantasy life—the same set of erotic fantasies that later in life led Lawrence to hire a fellow soldier to beat him with a birch rod.

To the common insistence that such beatings, even when to the point of orgasm, cannot "really" be called homosexuality (or perhaps even sexuality), Wolfe brilliantly asks, "Can anyone believe that to T. E. Lawrence, either the sex of the person beating him or the fact of his orgasm was unimportant? Or is sex only defined when genital meets genital, or as a process that involves pleasure but no pain?" These are crucial, difficult questions that linger long in the mind.

Perhaps still more remarkably, Wolfe refuses to be judgmental or moralistic about Lawrence's orgasmic preferences, or to account for them simply as the result of his "shame" over his homosexual impulses. Instead, Wolfe eloquently suggests that Lawrence's association of pleasure with pain was precisely what had made him into a "hero" in the first place—had made it possible for him to "go without food or sleep for days, to endure great thirst, or ride until his camel dropped."

Wolfe leaves open the question of whether Lawrence's undoubted erotic attraction to men automatically qualifies him as "gay"—though no better word or category seems available. In the same way, Wolfe acknowledges that although we have no certain proof of what Lawrence did or did not do in the bedroom—we almost never do for a historical figure—we have quite enough incidental evidence to confidently say that his orientation was unquestionably homoerotic.

The better question to ask, Wolfe suggests, is why heterosexual biographers of T. E. Lawrence have, in the first place, labored so long and hard to deny the essential fact of his erotic attraction to members of his own gender.

CHAPTER ONE

MOVIE-SCREEN MAGIC

The sellout crowd that poured into Covent Garden Royal Opera House during the week of August 14, 1919, was the most glamorous and glittering that London had seen in years. Dukes and lords, military heroes, scholars, and society figures had all turned out—not for opera, but to hear a real-life saga filled with every bit as much self-sacrifice, suffering, and heroism. The story's narrator was a journalist from Ohio in the United States, Lowell Thomas, whose "illustrated travelogue" had already played to capacity crowds at New York's Madison Square Garden. The actors were the wartime heroes of the large rectangular peninsula the British called Arabia: site of the garden of Eden, birthplace of Christianity, Judaism, and Islam, and home to nomadic warriors who rode on racing camels and fine Arabian horses over belts of untracked desert sands.

That the actors in Thomas's travelogue were on film and not on stage only made his audience more excited.

The American journalist Lowell Thomas (center, in boots, with back to the camera) meets Prince Feisal in Aqaba in 1918. T. E. Lawrence (third from left, in white headdress) stands at Feisal's side. More than anyone else, it was Thomas who was responsible for the birth of the Lawrence legend.

The journalist's sensational narration, slides, and newsreel footage of the recently concluded world war, accompanied by a full orchestra, offered drama as enthralling as the stories of the Knights of the Round Table that the audience had been raised on. Thomas spoke of "the last great crusade," Britain's World War I fight against the Turks of the Ottoman Empire. He showed the first moving pictures of "the holy lands of Arabia" and captivated the crowd with tales of the British cavalry driving toward the exotic city of Damascus. He held his listeners spellbound with stories of the Bedouin raiders who rode at their side, camel-borne warriors who appeared out of the desert, rifles at the ready, to sweep away the soldiers of the Turkish garrisons.

For an audience exhausted by World War I, this was the war as it should have been. Europeans had heard too much about the western front, where thousands had been gassed to death by an enemy they never saw, and hundreds of thousands died trying to capture a few yards of barbed wire and mud. Fighting in Arabia meant swooping across a vast sea of sand, pushing the enemy over mountains and through deserts, riding until you could hardly stay in the saddle. On the European battlefields, modern technology—mines, tanks, airplanes, and poison gas—had mocked the best efforts of any individual, cutting down even the most accomplished soldiers and leaving little place for heroism. Thomas's battlefields, on the other hand, were lands where few cars had ever touched the soil, and where a hundred men on camels could take a town.

And who, listening to the quavering voice of the Irish tenor singing an interpretation of the Muslim call to prayer, or staring out over the moonlight-on-the-Nile stage set, could resist the mystery of the East? Thomas spoke of the holy city of Jerusalem, which Christians and Muslims had fought over for seven centuries, and of Mecca, the birthplace of the Muslim prophet Muhammad. Christians were not permitted to enter Mecca, but each year hundreds of thousands of Muslims made a pilgrimage to that sacred city, swaying down from Syria on camelback, or on foot, or crossing in boats over the Red Sea. Mecca's ruler, King Hussein Ibn Ali, had been held for years by the Turks in their capital city of Constantinople and had been forced to raise his four

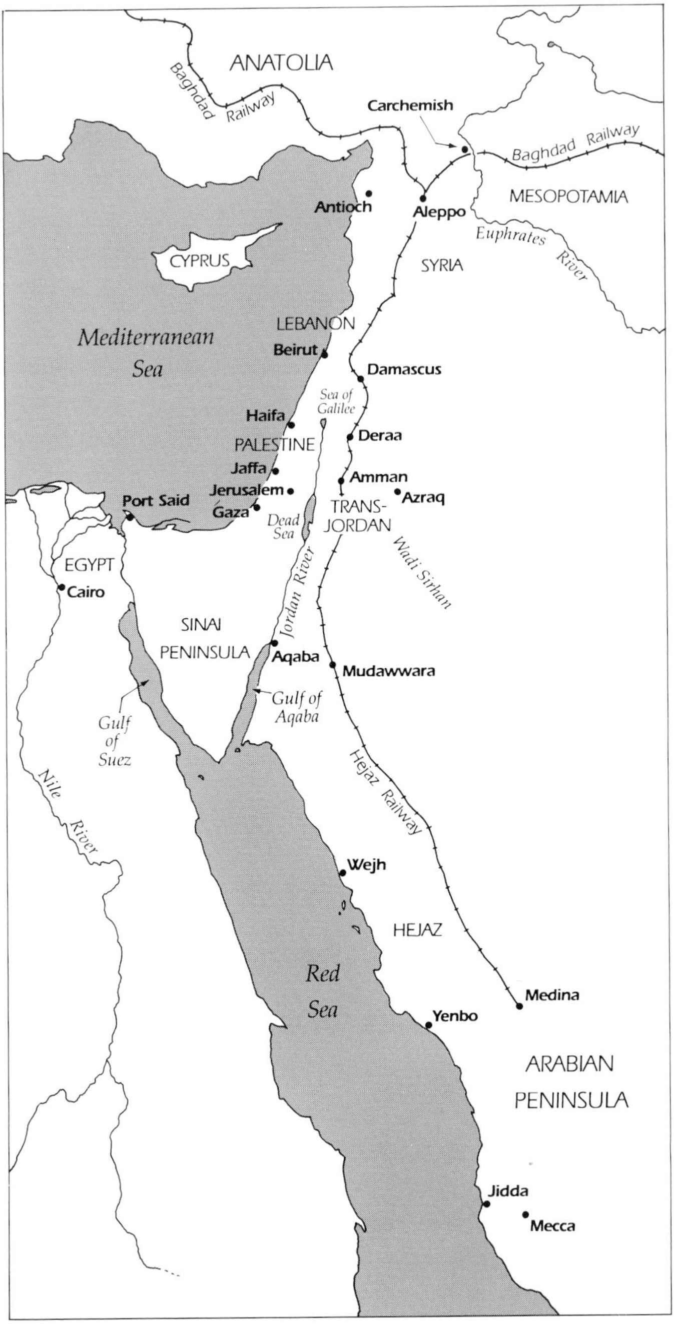

T. E. Lawrence's Middle East.

sons far from the desert. During World War I, Hussein's sons had each led separate bands of Bedouin in the fight for independence from the Turks, gathering momentum until the Arab bands had welded themselves into the right wing of the Allied army sweeping through Syria. Damascus had been taken, and Jerusalem, too, with General Edmund Allenby's forces walking through the gates of the city like the great crusaders of old. Thomas's story was one of victory, a triumph that left Britain in control of thousands of miles of new territories.

And his audiences loved it. The two-week run planned for Covent Garden lasted six months, and the king of England requested a special command performance. More than a million British citizens attended the lecture. But it was not the exotic dancers who performed the dance of the seven veils before the show began that moved the audience most. It was not the brilliant tactics of massive, square-jawed General Allenby of Palestine that captured their imagination. It was not King Hussein of Mecca, or his four sons, the princes Ali, Abdullah, Feisal, and Zeid.

Rather, it was someone smaller in stature who loomed largest in the popular imagination. He also rode on camelback, a five-foot-five figure clad in the white silk garments of a Meccan prince, riding at the head of a band of desert guerrilla fighters with the banner of the Arab revolt fluttering in the wind above him. He was English, though to that point few of his countrymen had heard of him. For a week after Thomas's opening performance, and for years afterward, the newspapers would be filled with stories and speculation about this mysterious blond-haired, blue-eyed man who would become perhaps the most celebrated hero of World War I.

Lawrence of Arabia. Terror of the Turks. Leader of the Arab revolt. Uncrowned king of the Arabs. Women and men wrote him love letters. Military experts idolized him, scholars sought his company, sculptors made statues in his likeness, and biographers wrote book after book about him. His own book would be a best-seller and a literary triumph, his activities the focus of every London tabloid. A slew of Hollywood movies about exotic Arabia—*The Sheikh, The Son of the Sheikh*—followed in his wake, as, much later, would a hit movie about Lawrence himself. "I deem him one of the greatest beings alive in our time," said Winston Churchill. "Whatever our need, we shall never see his like again."

So enraptured were the crowds by the images of this robed and daggered hero that no one noticed the small figure who slipped in several times to watch Thomas's show when the lights were out. But let *us* imagine him: a slender man of 31, with burning blue eyes and fair hair, clad perhaps in civilian clothes or the drab khakis of a British colonel, standing alone in the back. Does he blush and give a characteristic nervous giggle as he watches the crowd roar their approval at his bravery? Or is he serious, thinking about his Arab friends in the desert, for whom the fight for independence was not really over? This is a picture of Lawrence we see less often: Lawrence the man rather than Lawrence the hero.

Like Thomas's audience, history prefers the romantic image. But looking at Lawrence's life means undressing him, untwining the fantasies that, as surely as the gold cord round his head or the gold belt round his waist, keep his flowing white robes in place. Lawrence loved showmanship and tall tales, and many of the myths that veiled him were of his own making. Others were threads that ran through the fabric of life of his generation, and the generations that followed. So as you read, keep one eye on the real Lawrence: small and determined, but also restless, bruised, and dissatisfied. And remember also the striking, robed figure on the screen that Thomas first set up, and on which scores of adoring biographers have projected their own romantic fantasies. The story that unfolds there is a splendid one: of hot sands, love between men, battle, bravery, betrayal, and the Arab East.

CHAPTER TWO

AN IMPERIAL SON

Fate never played a stranger prank than when she transformed this shy young Oxford graduate . . . into the leader of a hundred thrilling raids, creator of Kings, Commander of an Army, and world champion trainwrecker.
—Lowell Thomas, *With Lawrence in Arabia,* 1924.

Sarah Lawrence with her four oldest boys, sometime around 1894. Young T. E., whom his family called Ned, is seated at left. Next to him stands William George, or Will. Frank is in his mother's arms; Montague Robert, known as Bob, stands at right.

T. E. Lawrence could be whatever you wanted him to be. Different people thought of him as an Englishman and an Arab, a scholar and a soldier, a man's man and a girlish boy, an athlete and an aesthete. John Buchan, adventure writer and politician, said he would have followed Lawrence "over the edge of the earth." Lionel Curtis, right-wing champion of English rule and royalty, greatly admired him, as did the socialist playwright George Bernard Shaw. Homophobic lovers of the limelight like Lowell Thomas found him irresistibly fascinating. So did the restrained homosexual geniuses of English letters E. M. Forster and W. H. Auden. Lawrence of Arabia has remained so famous after his death because in life he was able to play so many different, contradictory parts.

Lowell Thomas said it was fate that accounted for Lawrence's remarkable transformations. Westerners always seem to mention fate—Kismet—when they talk about the Middle East. But there are other, more fitting words to describe the forces that drove a young archaeologist with no military training to capture the city of Damascus and the imaginations of his countrymen. Other forces carried Lawrence along as a young student of medieval history and in his work as a mapmaker, spy, and soldier. One force shaped far more of the history of "Arabia," the territory we know now as the countries of Syria, Lebanon, Jordan, Israel, Iraq, Kuwait, Bahrain, Qatar, the United Arab Emirates, Yemen, and Saudi Arabia. And that force was not fate. It was Empire.

Thomas Edward Lawrence, known as Ned to his family and schoolmates, came into the world on August 15, 1888, smack in the middle of the great British imperial moment. He would later tell people that he had been born a day later, on Napoleon's birthday, which some said showed his ambition to be an emperor himself. But at the time of Lawrence's birth, imperial ambitions on the part of the European powers were the order of the day. Of all the empires known to history, the British Empire of the late 19th century, during the reign of Queen Victoria, was the largest. The Union Jack, as Britain's flag is known, flew over nearly one fifth of the surface of the earth and a quarter of its peoples. The huge country of India, where less than 75,000 British administered the affairs of 300 million Indians, was regarded as the empire's crown jewel, but there were many other, smaller gems: colonies and protectorates where the British traded, preached, and made sure that other, competing empires were kept away. Strung together, those gems became a necklace that circled the throat of the world, a network that England used to extend its power, and when necessary, to choke out threats to her influence. From Siam to Sudan, South Africa to Saskatchewan, the British sold their products, built their clubs, started their farms, trained the natives, advised the rulers, and extracted the wealth.

Lawrence's family roots were in less exotic and much closer imperial soil: Ireland. He was the second of five illegitimate sons born to Thomas Chapman, an Anglo-Irish aristocrat, and Sarah Junner, a governess who

Lawrence made this brass rubbing of William Viscount Beaumont from a medieval Essex church in 1905, during the course of a bicycle trip he took with his father. By "the age of 15," said his friend C. F. C. Beeson, "he was well versed in monumental brasses and had acquired a fine series of rubbings from churches in eastern and southern counties."

had come to Chapman's country mansion in Westmeath to take care of the four daughters he had with his wife. In a society whose gentlemen felt responsible both for enjoying their privileges and for setting a standard of propriety, it was not uncommon or unconscionable to keep a younger mistress—so long as you kept her a secret. But when a Chapman family butler discovered young Sarah living in a flat in Dublin, complete with a baby boy, Montague Robert, that Thomas had fathered, the scandal was not long in breaking, and Sarah and Thomas were forced to leave Ireland completely. At their first stop, a solid stone house in the village of Tremadoc in Wales, they changed their names. When their second son, Thomas Edward, was born later that year, the surname "Lawrence" went on his birth certificate.

If Lawrence became famous for living a double life, concealing his personal traits behind a public personality, he learned the basics at his parents' knees. Chapman's wife, Edith Hamilton, a woman so sour and sternly religious that locals called her "the vinegar queen" and "the Holy Viper," refused to grant her husband a divorce, so he and Sarah were never able to marry. Nor did Thomas and Sarah ever tell their children the story of their unconventional beginnings. T. E., who overheard his father talking to a lawyer one day about the name change, was the only one of the five boys who grew up knowing that he was illegitimate. This secret, with the secret of T. E.'s sexuality, would be folded together and carefully stored away by the rest of the Lawrence family. "God hates the sin but loves the sinner. God loves the sinner, but hates the sin," T. E.'s mother was heard to murmur deliriously on her deathbed. Whether she was talking about her own sins, or T. E.'s, the phrase—still painfully familiar to gay men and lesbians whose sex lives are not accepted by their deeply religious families—expresses the guilt that haunted both the religious mother and her much less religious son.

In daily life Sarah Lawrence was often heard murmuring prayers, and she faithfully attended the local churches, no matter where the family wound up in its search for a place to make a new life. Thomas and Sarah tried Scotland, where a third son, William George, was born in 1889. They went to northern France, where T. E. learned to speak French,

As a young man, Lawrence made himself an expert in the architecture of castles from the age of the Crusades. He considered this particular edifice, Crac des Chevaliers, to be "the finest castle in the world." Seen here is his own sketch of the west face of the inner ward, which he made sometime around his 21st birthday.

and to the Channel island of Jersey, where they had a fourth boy, Frank Helier. T. E. was seven before they finally settled in the English town of Oxford, where his youngest brother, Arnold, was born, and where all five boys would spend their childhoods. The home chosen by Thomas and Sarah, a four-floor brick house with a garden in the back, was like their relationship: new, and from the outside, solid and respectable.

Inside, too, the atmosphere was regular. Thomas Lawrence became a suburban, rather than a country, gentleman: riding a bicycle instead of horses, shooting photographs instead of bird guns, and living off the money he earned from his property back in Ireland. "My father never touched a book or a cheque," T. E. remembered later. Though Thomas

Lawrence's income was greatly diminished—he still had four children and a wife to provide for in Ireland, as well as Sarah and the five boys—he managed to send all the Lawrence boys to the modestly priced local day school. Each day the boys, dressed in identical striped jerseys and lined up according to age, would ride their bicycles down to the school. Forced by the unusual nature of their relationship to keep a low social profile, Thomas and Sarah had few friends and did little entertaining, so in some ways the family was a world unto itself. On Sundays, Sarah would lead them not once, not twice, but three times to the local Anglican Evangelical church. It was there, in bible class, that T. E. first heard the stories of the Holy Land in which he was to become famous.

What was there in this quiet existence that moved Lawrence to go abroad? Occasionally the flash of the jewels of the British crown lit up his suburban landscape, such as the day, when he was nine, that England celebrated the fiftieth anniversary of Queen Victoria's reign. On that day schoolchildren all over England, and in all the British colonies, celebrated the "Diamond Jubilee," for which they had rehearsed special songs and pageants that glorified Britain's imperial might. Lawrence was dressed in his finest clothes and taken to view the fleet, a collection of ships larger than all the other navies of the world combined, the backbone of Britain's power. In London crowds were awed by the procession of imperial sons that paraded down the streets: Indian Lancers in crimson breeches, dagger-carrying Gurkha soldiers from Nepal, Chinese police in straw hats, and English lords on prancing horses. Even as a schoolboy, Lawrence later wrote, he imagined himself as one of those imperial masters, "hustling into form, while I lived, the new Asia."

But more often the empire was lived, rather than learned or seen. It ran through Lawrence's daily life without really being visible, like the wires guiding the machinery of an elaborate stage set. The money that the Lawrence family lived on came from the Chapman estate in Ireland, which the English had ruled as a colony since the 16th century. The apples that the Lawrence boys ate for lunch came from Canada, which had been under exclusive British dominion since the 18th century;

their oranges, from Jamaica, which England had wrested from its original colonial overlords, the Spanish, in 1655; their mutton from New Zealand, which in the 1770s the great British explorer James Cook had been the first to describe in detail; their tea from India and Ceylon (now Sri Lanka), where the British had ousted the Dutch and the French more than a century earlier. The maps displayed in the classrooms of the Oxford High School showed Britain's colonies in red, as well as the red sea lanes down which the famous British warships moved. More than eight million English men and women had moved, too, gone to play a part in the administrative or commercial duties of the colonies. Everyone knew someone who had gone abroad. Even in quiet, staid Oxford the empire felt like a fantasy, part of a collective double life, an open door that offered escape from the cramped and rainy British isles.

And Lawrence, it seemed, was anxious for a way out. "All men dream, but not equally," he would write in his acclaimed autobiographical account of the Arab revolt, *Seven Pillars of Wisdom*. "Those who dream by night in the dusty recesses of their minds wake in the day to find that it was vanity, but the dreamers of the day are dangerous men, for they may act their dream with open eyes, to make it possible. This I did." Even as a boy, Lawrence was "dreamy," devouring stories of golden-haired knights and their quests to fight enemies and protect their family honor. Later, even as he was planning real battles, it was to this world of journeying, chivalrous warriors that he would retreat for strength and inspiration. British and Arab soldiers alike would recall him, a smile on his face, sitting in a tent and reading stories of King Arthur's Knights of the Round Table or Homer's *Odyssey*.

The real world, with its inevitable social complications and demands, offered less to the precocious Lawrence. School he found "an irrelevant and time-wasting nuisance." Cricket and other sports may have excited other boys, but Lawrence preferred going to old churches to make rubbings of the brass monuments, and to the library. He spent hours poring over descriptions of armor and coats of arms, and he joined the local archaeological society. He also taught Sunday school to younger children, though according to one account, that ended when he read

The five Lawrence brothers (from left, T. E., Frank, Arnold, Bob, and Will) in 1910. This is the last known photograph of them together.

them a story by Oscar Wilde. Wilde, known as one of the greatest wits and writers in England, had also been publicly tried and convicted for homosexual acts, which in those days were described as "Peccatum illude horrible, inter christanos non nominandum" (a sin so horrible it could not even be mentioned by Christians).

Lawrence never talked about his sexuality. If he was coming to realize that he shared Wilde's passions, he must also have learned from his example how dangerous it was to discuss them, let alone act upon them. In Victorian England, sexual relations outside of marriage were roundly condemned, and male homosexuality was a criminal offense. Homosexual intercourse was punishable by life imprisonment; even asking another man to have sex was punishable by two years of hard labor. So while other boys swore, made dirty jokes, or went to local fairs to find girls, Lawrence remained silent and removed. While other boys matched their bodies against each other in team sports, Lawrence practiced those he could do alone: gymnastics and running and bicycling. His brothers were meat eaters, but young T. E. spent several years as a vegetarian. Somewhere around the age of 16, Lawrence made his sense of separation clear by running away from home altogether, joining the army and forcing his father to come and buy him out.

For a time afterward, Lawrence confined his military interests to reading about warrior-adventurers: King Arthur, keeper of the Round Table; his most trusted adviser, the wizard Merlin; the illegitimate but pure young knight Galahad and his companion Percivale. Lawrence also enjoyed reading stories about the great real-life European crusaders who in the Middle Ages had sought to liberate the Holy Land from the Muslim infidels. His favorite was the homosexual king Richard Lion-Heart, who had been born in Oxford and was inseparable from his beloved friend and fellow crusader King Philip of France. Fascinated with fragments from Oxford's medieval past, Lawrence haunted construction sites in the area, offering workers a few pence for old glass and pottery. For three years in a row, he took long summer trips around England and France by bicycle in order to visit the castles built by the crusader kings. "By the time he was twenty, he had seen every twelfth century castle of importance in England, Wales, France,"

E. M. Forster wrote in an introduction to a volume of Lawrence's letters.

Those letters show Lawrence to be in many ways like the castles he studied: complex, fortified, and difficult to get inside. His small, lithe body grew muscled from the long trips, some over 100 miles a day, that he took on his special racing bike with the dropped handlebars. "Mme. Chaignon . . . got a shock when she saw my 'biceps' while bathing. She thinks I'm Hercules," he wrote in 1906 while on his first trip abroad, to France. In another he boasted that his "leg muscles are like steel now. I expect I'll delight Mother when I return. I'm brown as a berry." But an emotional steeliness often lay under Lawrence's pleasant tone, showing his reluctance to lower his personal defenses. "You want more details of myself; I really have none to give," he wrote his mother. To his father, he explained that "all my letters are equally bare of personal information. The buildings I try to describe will last longer than we will, so it is only fitting that they should have the greater space."

He carried a camera to photograph the monuments he visited, sketched them when he could, and memorized their architectural details. The more isolated he found himself, the better. "I love all waste/and solitary places where we taste/The pleasure of believing all we see/Is boundless, as we wish our soul to be," he wrote to his mother in a letter from France, quoting the poet Percy Bysshe Shelley. His other letters were filled with the poetry of William Blake and Alfred Lord Tennyson, the Greek phrases that were the mark of an educated English schoolboy, and aesthetic pronouncements that stressed his growing sense of himself as an expert. "That castle is quite above and beyond words," he wrote of one building. "It pollutes it to mention any but Chateau Gaillard, Pembroke and Caerphilly in the same breath."

But Lawrence's greatest praises were reserved for the sea, the simultaneous symbol of Britain's strength and isolation. He could hardly contain himself as he wrote home about catching his first glimpse of the Mediterranean, "when suddenly the sun leaped from behind a cloud, and a sort of silver shiver passed over the grey: then I understood and instinctively burst out with a cry of 'Thalassos, Thalassos! [the sea! the sea!]' that echoed down the valley and startled an eagle from the opposite hill. . . . Really this getting to the sea has almost overturned my mental balance: I would accept a passage to Greece tomorrow."

But it was not yet time. First Lawrence had to experience another rite of passage and gain admittance into one of the great learning centers that made it possible to move from England to the world of the classics. His eldest brother was already at Oxford University, and seven of the fourteen members of his high school class would go there. His own first attempt at gaining admission, to St. John's College, failed because his test scores were too low. He tried next for the less prestigious Jesus College, which offered special scholarships for people who had been born in Wales. His interview went well: he spoke with great authority about pottery collecting and brass rubbing, and by the summer of 1907 he had been accepted. He had just turned nineteen and was very relieved. "They drag those boy years out too much," he remembered later. "[W]hen after them I suddenly went to Oxford, the new freedom felt like Heaven."

CHAPTER THREE

LEARNING WHAT YOU'RE NOT

Here come I, my name is Jowett:
There's no knowledge but I know it.
I am the Master of this college.
What I know not isn't knowledge.

Those words were written to poke fun at a legendary Oxford don, but they were hardly a joke. The Oxford where Lawrence found himself in October of 1907 was one of the finest universities in the world, and certainly one of the most self-serious. For centuries students had put on black gowns, passed through Oxford's stone arches, and been lectured to by the dons who taught in the university's vast libraries, museums, and colleges. Upon graduation these fine young men of England had stretched themselves upward, like Oxford's famous stone spires, for the whole world to admire. The list of those who have studied at Oxford is a roll call of some of the most famous men in history: Sir Walter Raleigh and Sir Richard Burton, the poets Percy Bysshe Shelley and T. S. Eliot, the

Lawrence himself (standing at right) took this photograph of his classmates at the City of Oxford High School for Boys in July 1907. He used rubber tubing to connect his camera and tripod to his bicycle pump, which he hid behind his leg and used to trip the camera.

writers Evelyn Waugh and C. S. Lewis, dozens of English prime ministers, and U.S. president Bill Clinton, to name only a few.

"Gentlemen" was the word used in Lawrence's day to refer to young men at Oxford, and many would have expected to be addressed that way before arriving at the university. The sons of the richest families of England, these students had come from the poshest English boarding schools to take up residence in the oak-doored rooms of the Oxford colleges. Each of Oxford's many colleges was a separate institution with a separate character, though in virtually all of them the blazer-clad young Oxonians—discussing life over cigars and hot wine—moved about as surely as some would later take their place in Parliament. Fifty years before Lawrence's arrival, when scholarship students were not yet allowed, the wealthier undergraduates called upon as many as six servants to attend them. Time had brought students from the lower classes to Oxford, but the hallmarks of wealth remained: racehorses, hounds, hunting ponies, and an unquestioned sense of entitlement.

It was this rarefied environment that T. E. Lawrence—shy, short, on scholarship, and fresh from the city day school—entered in 1907. The transition from "Town" to "Gown" was a socially difficult one for Lawrence, particularly since after the first term he moved from rooms in college to a bungalow at the back of his family garden. His small size, habit of blushing and emitting a high-pitched, nervous giggle ("Tee Hee Lawrence," a satirist would later call him), and dislike for team sports further separated him from his more robust and conventional colleagues. "You Welshmen do seem to have the knack of picking the queerest fish," said one Oxford "gentleman" to another, who had made the social mistake of inviting Lawrence up to his rooms. "I know he's barmy. He doesn't run with the boats, he doesn't play anything. He just messes about on that awful drop-handled bicycle. And if he ever wore a bowler hat he'd wear it with brown boots."

In fact, if Lawrence had any interest in wearing a bowler hat, he probably would have worn it with a chain-mail shirt. For him, Oxford was a place to pursue his passion for medieval history and costume and for the stories that brought them to life. It was not long before he knew every legend and landmark associated with the medieval campus: how

King Alfred had founded the first college over a thousand years before; the tower where the horn of a unicorn was still supposedly kept; the names of the knights painted on the walls of the library of the Oxford Union. It was in that library that Lawrence, who steadfastly avoided the campus dining halls, nourished his mind, checking out the maximum number of books under his own name and then using his father's name to check out more. From there Lawrence would jump on his bicycle and pedal back to his bungalow, reading all night among the life-size rubbings of knights, priests, and other medieval characters he had hung on the wall. Friends dropping by his sparely furnished bungalow often found him stretched out on the floor, reading three or four books at the same time page by page. "It's lovely after you have been wandering in the forest with Percivale or Sagramors le Desirous [characters in Arthurian and medieval romances], to open the door . . . and look at the sun glowering through the valley mists," Lawrence wrote. "[I]f you can get the right book at the right time you taste joys—not only bodily, physical but spiritual also, which pass one out above and beyond one's miserable self."

In everyday life as well, Lawrence separated himself from the routine. One night, after reading a 17th-century account of an underground Oxford waterway called the Trill Mill Stream, Lawrence went out, found it, and poled his way through it in a small boat. When visiting the dorm rooms of his colleagues, Lawrence was known to sit for hours on the floor, smiling and listening without saying a word. At other times, as his friend Vivyan Richards recalled, he spent hours sitting naked in front of a peat fire in the bungalow, "placidly drawing his own foot and leg." Lawrence found modernity and industrialism disturbing, and he made no secret of his classical aesthetics. When the most accomplished athletes set off for the playing fields, Lawrence would follow solemnly behind, explaining to them the merits and deficiencies of their bodies as judged by the Greek standard of physical excellence.

Not every Oxford man found such behavior "barmy." Richards, a dark-haired philosophy student who was two years older than Lawrence, invited him to his rooms and promptly fell madly in love

The celebrated English artist Augustus John drew this portrait of David Hogarth for the original edition of *Seven Pillars of Wisdom*. Hogarth was mentor, patron, friend, and father figure to Lawrence. "He was very wise for others, and very understanding, and very comfortable," Lawrence said of Hogarth, "for he knew all the world's vices and tricks and shifts and evasions and pretexts, and was kindly towards them all."

with him. The two spent virtually every day together, meeting in Lawrence's bungalow and talking long into the night about their idol, the artist-craftsman William Morris, who had attempted a revival of various medieval arts and crafts. Morris, who died in 1896 at the age of 62, had studied and lived in Oxford, creating beautiful tapestries, stained-glass windows, and paintings about the lives of the knights, and then moved to the woods to build a medieval-style hall and hand-run printing press. Richards and Lawrence decided to do the same someday, with Lawrence even getting some money from his father to buy some 14th-century wooden beams for the project. With Richard Green, another Oxonian, Lawrence fantasized about living in a windmill by the sea and building a press on which they would publish their own and other people's writing about art and beauty.

For each of these young men, the dream of printing their own books held a special appeal, since none of the books that mainstream publishers produced seemed to describe them. Richards and Green were both homosexual, though if they or Lawrence had done what many young gay men and lesbians have done since and looked that word up in the dictionary to see if it applied to them, they would have been frustrated to find no listing at all. As the English writer Neil Bartlett has noted, the word homosexual, only recently invented, was not common enough to even be listed in the "complete" *New English Dictionary* of the time. The word "love" in that dictionary was defined as "the passionate attachment of two members of the opposite sex." The word "gay" was slang for being a prostitute and had nothing whatsoever to do with loving people of the same gender. There were other words, such as "invert" or "sodomite" or "Uranian," that people used to describe men who had sex with men, but those were not words that people like Lawrence or Richards would ever use about themselves. There were mail-order pamphlets with ridiculous "see-if-you're-a-Uranian" tests—one telltale sign was an inability to whistle—but Lawrence and his friends were too sophisticated for those. No wonder, then, that these young men fastened on the idea of producing their own publications, ones that expressed certain, perhaps forbidden, feelings in a language that they could understand.

But if Lawrence recognized his friends' passions for books as a stand-in for other kinds of passions, he did not explicitly reveal his own. Perhaps, like many college-age gays and lesbians today, he felt too afraid of the consequences. Even later, when Lawrence's Oxford friends felt moved to express their longing for male bodies, Lawrence was not able to follow. Richard Green's homoerotic poems, *Dream Comrades and Youthful Lovers,* would be published, but not by Lawrence. And years after Lawrence's death, Vivyan Richards would speak frankly to Lawrence biographers Phillip Knightley and Colin Simpson about the bittersweetness of always wanting to sleep with Lawrence and not knowing if he wanted to do the same. "If he had any similar feelings, he didn't let on," Richards told them. "I realize now that he was sexless—at least that he was unaware of sex."

But was Lawrence unaware of his body's urges, or simply determined to discipline them? Lawrence's love of art, or of men, would never translate into the velvet wearing or lily carrying that led the fascist Oswald Mosely to refer to some of Lawrence's colleagues as "the shimmying half men of Oxford." Lawrence's distinctiveness was a Puritan kind, resting more on showy displays of what he did *not* do than on what he did. While others sipped on hot wine or whiskey, Lawrence never drank. While others ate at the dining hall, Lawrence nibbled on a few biscuits or fasted. He walked his bicycle downhill and rode it up, and forced himself to swim in the icy river in the middle of winter. Even sleep was too soft for Lawrence: he would stay up for days in a row, then go to bed in a box of hard boards, shaped like a coffin, with no pillow. Lawrence found other kinds of discipline in the Officers Training Corps and in the hours he spent shooting a revolver until he was equally good with either hand.

This mix of medievalism and military self-discipline may have mystified Lawrence's refined friends, but it caught the eye of a teacher. For D. G. Hogarth, the keeper of the Ashmolean Museum, where Lawrence had a job neatening display cases, Lawrence's medieval style had distinctly modern possibilities. Hogarth, a bearded 47-year old don at Magdalen College, had worked as a journalist and archaeologist in Greece, Cyprus, and the Middle East before taking his post at Oxford. With his command of Middle East politics and customs and his strong belief that the British Empire should continue to expand, Hogarth would become a mentor for Lawrence, a man he would call "the parent I could trust, without qualification, to understand what bothered me."

Details about much of Hogarth's work remain sketchy, and there is good reason to believe he wanted it that way. Hogarth had a double life of his own—he was both a scholar and a spy, gathering information about different countries for the British government. But where Lawrence's secrets made him feel like an illegitimate outsider, Hogarth moved through the world with a sense of belonging. Lawrence was amazed at the ease with which the self-possessed don could switch from French to German, Italian to Greek, and Turkish to Arabic. Hogarth changed social settings just as easily, maintaining close relationships with many of the explorers, generals, and foreign secretaries who were the empire's celebrities. Perhaps Lawrence felt himself drawing closer to that glamour when Hogarth invited him to join the small group of undergraduates who came to the don's house for discussions on military history. It was study with a purpose, for Hogarth would later invite many of those present, including Lawrence, to take part in his military intelligence work.

University students today may protest against the presence of the Central Intelligence Agency on college campuses, but in those days of the British Empire, spying was the work of a gentleman. "Uncivilized regions of the earth should be annexed or occupied by advanced

Lawrence (seated, front row, at left) was one of the first volunteers for the Oxford University Officers Training Corps, which was established in 1908. This photograph was probably taken in 1910. He later indicated that nothing that he learned in the corps proved of any use to him in wartime.

powers," advised the 1894 *Chapters on the Principles of International Law.* Hogarth, whose methods placed educated Englishmen across the globe, was doing things by the book. He gave students practice at being conquerors: assigning readings in military history, helping Lawrence and others argue strategy, and advising them as they refought famous battles from all different sides.

It was the poet and novelist Rudyard Kipling—who won the Nobel Prize for Literature the year Lawrence entered Oxford—who best gave voice to the conquering spirit behind Lawrence's education. In his novel *Kim,* Kipling cast a spell over England with the story of an Anglo-Irish boy trained as a spy in the "Great Game" of imperial espionage in India. In the course of the novel Kim slips constantly between Western and Eastern dress, makes long journeys in disguise, speaks fluently in native languages, and brings the mysteries of the East to life. Enigmatic British experts, much like Hogarth, oversee Kim's education and teach him his spying skills. For Kim, espionage and adventure are little more than an extension of his childhood pranks, yet with every triumph—every map he makes, every native he outsmarts, every agent from another country that he outmaneuvers—the grand mission of the British Empire is advanced. Later, after World War I, many would see Lawrence's story as something out of the pages of a novel like *Kim.*

But picture Lawrence and the others gathered round Hogarth, and another real-life story also comes to mind. It is the story of Burgess, Philby, Blunt, and McLean, young men who were Cambridge colleagues in the 1930s and who all would later work as spies for the Soviets. England would be scandalized to find that these members of the social and diplomatic elite—Blunt was an adviser to the queen, and Philby was one of the highest-ranking members of British intelligence—were Communist agents, and in many cases homosexual. Was it, many wondered, their sexuality—their "criminal nature"—that made them traitors? They should have asked if it was homophobia that made the men so good at espionage. Spies and homosexuals, after all, need the same skills: the ability to go undercover, to fight fear of disclosure, to talk in self-protective innuendo and scan for signs of receptivity. Did Hogarth's eyes, moving across his living room, spy out young Lawrence's untapped potential? Or was it Lawrence who used Hogarth, finding in that familiar gaze a way out of a world in which he felt ashamed?

In 1909, with Hogarth's support, Lawrence went off to explore Syria. He went to study, not to spy, and that summer, armed with a pistol, a camera, and a small sack of clothes, he walked over 1,000 miles. He returned, feet bleeding and blistered, to regale his friends with stories: being robbed by a bandit, being stricken with malaria, and seeing the glory of 37 different castles from the days of the crusades. With characteristic self-assurance, Lawrence had also returned with a startling conclusion: that the crusader castles in Syria had been built following the European example, rather than the other way around. It was an extremely unorthodox argument, one that most experts would disagree with today, but it was well enough argued to earn Lawrence a prized First in history.

Later to be published as the book *Crusader Castles,* Lawrence's thesis also showed Hogarth that Lawrence had what it took to be a British agent—a belief in the superiority of British civilization and a love of danger. Lawrence's tales of his trip would grow more embroidered every time he told them—he was soon claiming to have shot a bandit through the hand, to have traveled to villages where he was the first European visitor, to have fended off a mob with a revolver in one hand and a camera in the other. The stories may not have been true, but they revealed a truth: travel offered Lawrence an even better way of getting out of the repressive present than reading did. When Hogarth's college offered Lawrence a small scholarship to work with the don on an archaeological site, he accepted immediately. Their destination, Carchemish, Syria (on the west bank of the Euphrates River, in what is now south-central Turkey), would suit both men—Hogarth the spy master and Lawrence the dreamer—perfectly.

CHAPTER FOUR

LOVE IN THE EAST

Interview young men from the surrounding villages, and decide who will have work and who will not. Divide the laborers into groups, making sure that feuding families are kept separate. Command that quarreling workmen be locked up until they come to their senses. Practice shooting until you can hit a matchbox at thirty paces. And at the end of the day, dressed in spotless white flannel with a white and gold embroidered waistcoat, settle down to a meal, prepared by a manservant, that includes a choice of three blends of tea and nine varieties of jam. The life of an English knight or feudal lord? No, the life of 26-year-old T. E. Lawrence on the archaeological dig in Carchemish.

Lawrence took this photograph of his friend Salim Ahmed, or Dahoum, at Carchemish in 1911. "I had wrought for him freedom to lighten his sad eyes: but he had died waiting for me," Lawrence later wrote of Dahoum.

For a young man who had so often been reminded of his relative poverty at Oxford, the situation in Syria was a welcome relief. The caravan Hogarth and Lawrence accompanied to Carchemish included twenty supply camels and mules. And whether reading leatherbound volumes in front of the fire at night or cataloging ancient Hittite artifacts during the day, Lawrence was certainly living more luxuriously than

Lawrence (left) with Leonard Woolley at the dig in Carchemish in 1913. Woolley was impressed with Lawrence's ability as an archaeologist, if sometimes puzzled by his personality: Lawrence "would make brilliant suggestions but would seldom argue in support of them," he said. "They were based on sound enough argument, but he expected you to see these for yourself, and if you did not agree he would relapse into silence and smile."

he could have at home. The archaeologists' "hut" was furnished with white leather armchairs that Lawrence had made to order in the town of Aleppo. Its floor was a Roman mosaic that they had excavated while unearthing the older Hittite items below. Their bathtub was a basin of beaten copper, and their teacups were made of 4,000-year-old Hittite clay. Hogarth returned to Oxford after a year, but Lawrence was happy to stay on in Syria. "I feel [like I am] on my native heath, and am on the pitch of settling in a new Carchemish as Sheik," Lawrence wrote home cheerfully.

The territory that the English called Syria in those days was much bigger than the present-day nation of the same name: it extended all the way from southern Turkey to the edge of the Sinai Peninsula and included the cities of Damascus, Beirut, and Jerusalem. There was not even an equivalent for the name "Syria" in Arabic, the language of most of the people who lived there: like the United States before they were united, different provinces had their own names, their own populations, and their own ways of life. The men who lived and worked with Lawrence on the site of the dig were Muslim peasants, but elsewhere in Syria were nomads and citydwellers, Christians and Jews, fair-haired Circassians and dark-eyed Kurds. Perhaps the one thing all these people had in common was that they were subjects of the Ottoman Turks, whose capital was in Constantinople and who had ruled the Middle East for more than 400 years.

Challenging Turkish power, and the power of the Germans who were the Ottomans' strongest allies, would be a theme that preoccupied Lawrence during all his time in the Middle East. At Carchemish, playing out colonial rivalries was as much a part of life as piecing together ancient pottery. When construction of a Berlin-to-Baghdad railway brought German workers onto the southern side of the archaeological site in 1912, Lawrence and Leonard Woolley—the Oxonian Hogarth had left in charge—immediately tried to buy the land out from under them. When the landowner refused, and Turkish authorities questioned Woolley's right to be excavating at all under Hogarth's permit, the Englishmen solved the problem with their revolvers. Storming into the police office, Lawrence at his side, Woolley informed the Turks that he would shoot any man who interrupted the dig. In the end the Germans built several feet away from the British land. And when a dispute between the Germans and their workers threatened to turn bloody, Lawrence and Woolley took out their revolvers again and rushed to the rescue. What better way of proving superiority than to save your rival?

Most amazing of all, this gunpoint diplomacy was completely legal. Under an agreement called the Capitulations, Europeans could do as they pleased in the Ottoman Empire, being accountable only to their country's consulates and not to the Turkish authorities. Lawrence reveled in his power, solving local disputes, feasting with tribal chiefs, and making sure his family knew about all of it. "I'm with Ned now, who's very well and a great lord in this place," his brother Will wrote as he passed through Carchemish en route to a teaching post in India. "When I saw him last . . . he was wearing white flannels, socks and red slippers with a white Magdalen blazer and was talking to the governor of Biredjik in a lordly fashion." Lawrence's accounts to his parents were filled with a sense of English invincibility. "Good Heavens, don't you know that no Turkish officer or policeman or government official can lay hands on an Englishman or enter his house?" he wrote. "There would be a warship in Beirut if anyone in Biredjik insulted us."

What made the British so much more effective than their imperial competitors, though, was that they relied so little on warships. As Minister of Information John Buchan would later put it, the British could "get inside the skin of the natives" better than anyone else on earth. The Germans painted numbers on the backs of their workers to keep track of them, but Lawrence prided himself on more sophisticated methods. He learned about the families and feuds of the men, acted as judge and marriage broker, and distributed money instead of the daily floggings doled out at the German camp. Fluency in Arabic, too, reinforced Lawrence's sense of himself as a benevolent ruler. "It strikes me that the strongly dialectical Arabic of the villagers would be as good as a disguise to me," Lawrence wrote to Hogarth in England, perhaps foreseeing his future course of action.

The "disguise," of course, was most important to Lawrence and the rest of the British. As Lawrence himself admitted later, no Arab ever mistook him for one of them: his accent was too bad and his eyes were too blue. But in Carchemish, Lawrence was learning the basics of what would later be his leadership philosophy. "Keep always on your guard, never say an unnecessary thing: watch yourself and your companions all the time: hear all that passes, search out what is going on beneath the surface, and keep everything you find out to yourself," Lawrence wrote later in a manual for undercover agents wishing to work with the Bedouin. It was advice that many gays and lesbians today will recognize: learn the rules of the others, and know how not to call attention to your differences.

But paradoxically enough, learning to blend in at Carchemish was bringing Lawrence closer to freedom of sexual expression. In Syria, far away from British concern with illegitimacy and sexual propriety, Lawrence enjoyed what would be his happiest years. For the first time, the object of his affections was not an object at all. It was at Carchemish that Lawrence met the greatest love of his life.

His name was Salim Ahmed, but everyone jokingly called him Dahoum, "the little dark one." Woolley remembered him as a boy of about fifteen, "beautifully built and remarkably handsome." When he met Lawrence, Salim's job was to lead the donkey that carried the water containers around to the thirsty workers. Shortly thereafter, he was promoted to houseboy and became Lawrence's constant companion. The two swam together, took photographs of each other, wrestled, shared food, language lessons, and their most intimate secrets. During the four years that he spent at Carchemish, Lawrence made frequent excursions to other areas of the Middle East, often accompanied by Dahoum, whom he once even brought home with him to visit his family in England.

"I loved you, so I drew these tides of men into my hands," Lawrence wrote years later in "To S. A.," the poem that opens *Seven Pillars of Wisdom*. "And wrote my will across the sky in stars/To earn you Freedom, that seven pillared, worthy house/That your eyes might be shining for me, when we came." Later, when asked why he had helped launch a revolt that had given the Arabs a belief in their right to self-determination, Lawrence's response was a simple one: "I liked a particular Arab very much, and thought that freedom for his race would be an acceptable present."

In those early years in Syria, though, Dahoum was freeing Lawrence. The young men would exchange clothes, Lawrence wearing Dahoum's Arab skirt and vest and Dahoum donning shorts and red slippers. In summertime, when work on the dig stopped, Dahoum and Lawrence, both in native dress, would wander the countryside together. In *Seven*

Pillars, Lawrence describes how Dahoum brought him to a ruined palace made by a prince for his queen. The "clay of the building was said to have been kneaded for greater richness, not with water, but with the precious essential oils of flowers," Lawrence writes. "My guides, sniffing the air like dogs, led me from crumbling room to room, saying 'This is jasmine, this violet, this rose.' But at last, Dahoum drew me. 'Come and smell the very sweetest scent of all,' and we went into the main lodging, to the gaping window . . . and there drank with open mouths of the effortless, empty, eddyless wind of the desert, throbbing past."

When Woolley was away, Lawrence took advantage of his absence to have Dahoum come live with him in the expedition hut, where he had the young man pose naked for a sculpture that he carved out of soft limestone. The locals were scandalized when Lawrence set the figure on the roof. It was probably not intense, romantic relations between young men that so shocked them: it is still not uncommon, in many parts of the Arab world, for unmarried boys to sleep together. Older Arab men, too, often have homosexual sex: so long as they play the "active" role in anal intercourse and do not speak publicly about it, the behavior is accepted as a part of life. But for Lawrence to put up a sculpture of his naked young lover violated both the Muslim prohibition against figurative art and the unspoken norm of all sexual conduct in the Middle East: in affairs of the body, extreme discretion is required.

And respect for those norms was precisely what love for Dahoum was instilling in Lawrence. Sending to a nearby school for books for his new friend, whom he had already taught a few words of English, Lawrence asked for "nothing with a taste of Farangi [European]" influence. By the summer of 1912, Lawrence had come to feel that he was the pupil. "The foreigners come out here always to teach, whereas they very much better learn, for in everything but wits and knowledge the Arab is generally the better man of the two," he wrote. ". . . [T]he perfectly hopeless vulgarity of the half-Europeanised Arab is appalling. Better a thousand times the Arab untouched."

Lawrence (left) and Dahoum. The photographs are believed to have been taken in 1912 by Lawrence himself.

The ways in which Lawrence himself was touching Dahoum were not discussed, although the Englishman did take care of his Arab protégé when he fell ill with malaria, bathing him and sitting on his chest to keep him from shaking with fever. Dahoum returned the favor when Lawrence contracted a case of dysentery that left him so sick that the site foreman, Hamoudi, had to take Lawrence into his house. Dahoum came every day to nurse him, and in the summer of 1913 Lawrence took both him and Hamoudi home to England as a way of thanks. This time it was the Oxford neighbors who were shocked at the sight of the Arabs, both in their native garb, riding bicycles and going in and out of the garden. Lawrence seemed delighted and took Dahoum to a portrait painter to immortalize the visit.

We have no diaries of Dahoum's, no letters carefully preserved for history. What was the handsome young man thinking as he, one strong leg crossed over the other, stared out to the right of the frame, toward the East? Was he grateful or resentful that his companion, Lawrence, kept him from the crowds of people who flocked to photograph him and Hamoudi as the Arabs walked the city streets? Was he in love with Lawrence, or just a young, poor boy who saw in his British friend a chance at bettering his situation and seeing the world? Lawrence wanted Dahoum to remain pure, but what did Dahoum want? Was he happy to be in Arab dress in England? Or would he have preferred to slip into trousers, a blazer, and a bowler hat, blending in among these foreigners in the same way that Lawrence had immersed himself in the alien culture of the Arabs?

The dynamic between colonizer and colonized is often a complicated mix of domination, affection, oppression, and opportunity. Lawrence always saw himself as separate from his British fellows, a Lone Ranger. While in Syria, Dahoum was his Tonto, a native sidekick who, walking or riding at his side, showed him the ways of the land. Later, Dahoum would be the Holy Grail as Lawrence played Sir Galahad, a sacred image that inspired the young British knight as he rode into battle. Former British gunner Tom Beaumont, talking to Lawrence biographers Knightley and Simpson, would claim that Dahoum was also Lawrence's employee, a spy that Lawrence paid throughout much of the war to keep him advised of Turkish troop movements.

Lawrence and Dahoum both had their first taste of espionage in January 1914, when the two joined Woolley and Colonel Stewart Newcombe on a trip to map the Turkish-controlled Sinai Peninsula. Supposedly launched by a London exploration society interested in biblical history, the journey also had a military application. Any Ottoman attack on the Suez Canal, lifeline of the British trade route to India, would come across the Sinai, and the British needed to know the exact location of watering holes and routes that might be used by Turkish troops.

For six weeks the foursome mapped the Sinai desert. At Aqaba, the town on the border of the Sinai and Syria, a suspicious Turkish governor refused to allow them to photograph or examine anything, but Lawrence and Dahoum made sure they did both, even rigging together a raft from two empty tanks and paddling across shark-infested waters to explore a ruined crusader fort. When the governor sent out a Turkish squadron to investigate, the men eluded the soldiers, slipping safely back to Carchemish.

That summer, though, Lawrence would not be able to wander with his friend as he had grown into the habit of doing: the Turks were suspicious about the Sinai trip, and the British needed an archaeological report published "p.d.q." (pretty damn quick). Lawrence went off to London to finish the report, later published as *Wilderness of Zin,* while Dahoum was left in charge of the site.

It was an exceptionally warm, pleasant summer in England, and neither Lawrence nor many others saw it as what it was: the calm before a terrible, deadly storm. But by August 1914 imperial rivalries had blazed into armed conflict, and Europe was at war. France, England, and Russia sided together, while Germany and the Austro-Hungarian Empire opposed them. The Ottomans joined the German side in October. Syria, as Lawrence had known it, would be shattered by the conflict. Lawrence would never get to see Carchemish, or while away the hours with his beloved Dahoum, again.

CHAPTER FIVE

WARRIOR IN TRAINING

Dulce et decorum est por patria mori: It is sweet and right to die for one's country. Englishmen of Lawrence's generation, raised on this line of Latin, welcomed World War I with all the enthusiasm of a generation whose childhoods had been filled with stories of knights and empty of any direct experience of war. The fighting would end by Christmas, everyone was assured, and few men in the prime of life wanted to miss it. Lawrence's younger brother Frank, though still an undergraduate at Oxford, took a commission as an officer. Another brother, Will, rushed back from India to enlist in the armed forces. Troops from all over the empire came, too: Canadians and New Zealanders, Indians and Sudanese. "Much suff'ring shall cleanse thee," Poet Laureate Robert Bridges wrote to the young men flooding the recruiting offices, "but thou through the flood/Shall win to salvation, to Beauty through blood."

In transition: Lawrence in Arab headdress and the uniform of a British soldier.

How much more blood than beauty there would be in World War I would soon become obvious. The golden-haired lads of England and the patriots from the colonies found themselves not galloping through wooded glades but packed together in the trenches that the opposing armies gouged into the face of Europe. The trenches, dug out of crumbling earth and held together with sandbags and iron, ran in miles of zigzags to protect the men inside from shelling. But military technology had outstripped conventional military strategy. Instead of shells, the newest weapon—poison gas—killed thousands as they huddled in the underground hallways. When either side's forces set aside the periscopes they used to see out and went "over the top" and into battle, another new weapon—the machine gun—mowed them down in mind-boggling numbers. At the battle of the Somme, over a million casualties were suffered in four and a half months of fighting. When British cavalry and tanks were ordered to charge through a swamp, thousands of men and pack animals drowned in the mud.

Lawrence, whom Hogarth had gotten a job as a mapmaker in the London war office, would never see the European trenches. For one thing, he was too small: the recruiting offices would not take him. For another, he was needed to help defeat the Turks, who were trying to convince the more than 70 million Muslims all over the Middle East and South Asia to join their fight against the British. "Drive them out! If they attack you, slay them! Such is the reward for unbelievers!" Sultan Mehmed V of the Ottoman Empire urged his fellow Muslims. As a propaganda measure, the Germans announced that the kaiser had converted to Islam, changing his name to Guilliam Haji. This was a modern Holy War, a crusade, and it was to help plan a response that Britain dispatched the newly commissioned Captain T. E. Lawrence to Cairo, Egypt, in December 1914.

Carchemish had offered rural charms, but Cairo was a modern metropolis, complete with boulevards, electric tramways, and grand hotels. The cosmopolitan setting was matched by equally cosmopolitan company for Lawrence: the intelligence operation where he would spend the next two years was the brains rather than the brawn of the British presence in Egypt and was staffed by the most brilliant Middle

East hands that England could assemble. Lawrence was the youngest of them; his colleagues were journalists, butterfly collectors, military men, and members of Parliament who had spent years in the region. Hogarth passed through often, first as a roving spy, and later as the head of the new Arab Bureau for which Lawrence would work. Woolley, Lawrence's colleague from Carchemish, and Colonel Newcombe from the Sinai expedition were often seen going up the front stairs of the Savoy Hotel, where intelligence had its offices. Up the back stairs came what Lawrence called the "nasty network" of spies: smugglers, expatriates, industrialists, and members of high society willing to exchange information for British gold.

"Our Intelligence . . . is a very superior sort of thing," Lawrence wrote to Hogarth shortly after his arrival, and even Lawrence's first posting as a minor mapmaker did little to dampen his enjoyment of that superiority and the accompanying opportunity for nonconformity. Trained military men wore spotless uniforms, but Lawrence seldom bothered, preferring to stay long-haired, beltless, and rumpled. His colleague and former member of Parliament Aubrey Herbert was even more eccentric, going about in a canary yellow outfit made of curtain fabric, a Turkish hat, and slippers. In Lawrence's case, disdain for dress codes was coupled with a disrespect for the military rule of deference to one's superiors. When he found two older, more experienced mapmakers transliterating Roman names in a way that he thought incorrect, he did not hesitate to let them know exactly how mistaken they were. "Who," one of them is said to have inquired after the lecture, "is this extraordinary pipsqueak?"

Very few people knew: still not a drinker or a socialite, Lawrence preferred to pass his evenings quietly reading Latin and Greek in the home of the fastidious Sir Ronald Storrs. As "Oriental Secretary," Storrs was one of the highest-ranking British officials in Egypt, a trained classicist who spoke impeccable Arabic and was well able to match Lawrence's opinionated pronouncements on aesthetics with a few of his own. Usually, though, Lawrence read alone: Storrs, like most of Lawrence's upper-crust colleagues in Egypt, was more often found smoking Turkish cigarettes on the well-manicured lawns of the foreigners-only Turf Club, passing time at the polo fields, or relaxing in his box at the Cairo Opera House. At night, many British plotted battles from the bar of the famous Shepheard's Hotel, where Europeans often came to costume balls dressed as Egyptians.

Even when war came close, British Cairo retained its party atmosphere. "[I hear that] the Turks are to bring thousands of camels down to the Canal and then set a light to their hair," Herbert wrote to a friend from Shepheard's after the British rebuffed a Turkish attempt on the Suez Canal in February 1915. "The camel, using its well-known reasoning powers, will dash to the Canal to put the fire out. When they have done this in sufficient quantities the Turks will march over them."

It was in this mood of jolly nonchalance that Herbert and others among Lawrence's colleagues joined the Allied forces preparing to storm the Turkish capital of Constantinople. The plan was simple: land forces on Gallipoli (the thin peninsula that extends into the Aegean Sea on the north side of the Dardanelles), fight up and over the rocks to capture the forts guarding the narrow straits of the Dardanelles, and let the Royal Navy steam triumphantly up that waterway toward Constantinople. Clearing the southern half of Gallipoli was supposed to take three days, historian Jan Morris has noted, and soldiers armed with tourist guides to Asia Minor left Cairo in droves to join up. "The poor old Turkish Empire is only hanging together by a thread," Lawrence wrote to his parents in April, only a few weeks before the operation. He decided to remain in Cairo, however, noting that it did not seem appropriate to go off to the war with no field training.

In fact, no training could have prepared Lawrence or any other British soldier for the colossal failure of Gallipoli. Interrogating prisoners of war and talking to wounded soldiers sent back to Egypt's hospitals, Lawrence heard the full, sordid story of what historians would call the greatest reversal suffered by the British army since the successful revolt of the 13 American colonies. Nine months after the offensive began, the Turks were still squarely in control of the Dardanelles. On some beaches British soldiers had been mowed down before they even got out of their boats. Thousands of corpses were lying, blackened, stinking, and unburied, between the British and Turkish lines. And the Turks

Lawrence (left) confers with Hogarth (center), head of the Arab Bureau of British intelligence in Cairo, as Colonel Alan Dawnay looks on. One Arab who knew Lawrence in Cairo, Abd al-Rahman Shahbandar, found that his genuine interest in the Arabs set him apart from other British intelligence officers: "It appears to me that this man is different from the rest of the Englishmen we have seen so far, that he listens attentively . . . and that his questions show a depth in the subject which is not present except with one who has in it a pleasure and a passion."

were striking back, too, in Mesopotamia (an ancient region around the Tigris and Euphrates rivers, contained now within the borders of the present-day nation of Iraq), where they had surrounded 10,000 British soldiers and were starving them into surrender.

If Lawrence felt any guilt about not participating in the British operations at Gallipoli, it must have grown stronger after getting word that his brothers Frank and Will had both been killed in battle on the western front. "We cannot all go fighting," he wrote to his mother defensively after Frank's death in May 1915. But with a friend at the Ashmolean Museum, he was more candid. "They were both younger than I am," he wrote, "and it doesn't seem right that I should go on living peacefully in Cairo."

In fact, Lawrence would not continue to live peacefully. Instead, the pipsqueak began to squeak louder, joining Hogarth and others in Cairo who were arguing for a new military strategy. If the British were having trouble fighting the Turks directly, Lawrence believed, they should get Arab leaders to fight for them. The Turks may have shared a religion with the Arabs, but they were not willing to share power, and Lawrence was sure that with a little coaxing the Arabs would rebel against their Muslim oppressors.

Lawrence's first attempt to stir up a rebellion, on a trip he took to Mesopotamia, met with little interest from the local Arab leadership, but there were other possibilities. Sharif Hussein of the holy city of Mecca, for example, as a descendant of the Prophet Muhammad, was both a respected political and religious leader. Why not have him spearhead a revolt against Turkish domination in the Middle East? If "properly handled," Lawrence wrote in January 1916, the Arabs would combine to drive out the Turks, but would be incapable of standing together against the British. There was an added advantage to the scheme—if it succeeded, it would allow England to edge out even its most friendly colonial competitors in the region. Supporting an Arab revolt might allow the British to "biff the French out of all hope of Syria," Lawrence put it frankly to Hogarth, though obviously the British Command could not openly admit, at the risk of imperiling wartime unity, the appeal of winning out over its most important ally.

Lawrence was calling for the use of insurgency, one of the most basic and important tools of intelligence work in the 20th century. Today, supporting local opposition to destabilize a government you dislike is standard practice for secret agents. American spies in the 1980s, for example, used such a strategy in Nicaragua to build up the contras and in Afghanistan to build up the mujahideen. In the great days of the British Empire, though, the idea seemed especially threatening, because in order to get people to fight for themselves you had to promise them freedom. And that promise, according to officials in the British colonial bureaucracy, might turn native populations into "Frankenstein monsters" that could not be controlled after the war. "It is highly inexpedient and unnecessary to put into the hands of the backward people of the country what seem to us the visionary and premature notions of the creation of an Arab state," an alarmed Indian Office cabled to Cairo in November 1915.

Still, Lawrence and his superiors in Egypt carried the argument. The British promised Sharif Hussein of Mecca independence after the war if he rose up against the Turks. And in June 1916, Hussein stuck a rifle through the window of his palace and fired a symbolic shot at the nearby Turkish barracks. Led by his four sons, with support from British warships, Hussein's armies rose up against the Turks at cities all over what is now Saudi Arabia. Mecca was taken. The ports of Jedda and Yenbo were taken. Hogarth and Storrs were among the British experts who rushed over to offer advice, guns, and trained Egyptian soldiers to support the effort. Still a junior officer, Lawrence had to content himself with supervising the production of a new postage stamp with Hussein's face on it.

But the Arab revolt sparked one inside Lawrence as well. He had a leave coming to him in October of 1916. Instead of going to London, he went the other way and joined Storrs, who was en route back to Jedda to advise the revolt. Lawrence of Arabia was about to be born.

CHAPTER SIX

CROSSING THE BARRIER

If Dahoum the donkey boy had stopped Lawrence's heart, Feisal, son of Hussein, got it beating again. Lawrence's face was blistered from days of hard riding in the hot sun; his eyes were streaming and swollen. Yet from the moment that his guides halted their camels and led him to the long, low house in the oasis, Lawrence felt he could see the future. For there—a tall, slender white figure, guarded by a sword-bearing slave—stood Feisal.

Feisal's eyes, Lawrence wrote in *Seven Pillars,* were "dark and appealing." He was 31, only three years older than Lawrence, and his body was "tall, graceful and vigorous," with "a royal dignity to his head and shoulders." Lawrence's military report of the time compared Feisal to his childhood hero, Richard Lion-Heart. In *Seven Pillars,* Lawrence was even more fulsome in his praise: "I felt at first glance that this was the man I had come to Arabia to seek—the leader who would bring the Arab revolt to full glory," he wrote.

Lawrence (right) in the desert with two unidentified Arab companions.

The "glory" of Hussein's revolt, Lawrence had soon discovered, had been much easier to imagine in Cairo than to find in Arabia. In theory, the province over which Hussein had influence—the Hejaz, or Barrier—was enormous; the region of the Arabian Peninsula along the Red Sea included Mecca and Medina, the holiest cities of Islam, to which all Muslims try to make a pilgrimage at least once in their lives. But as the starting point for a rebellion, Hussein's territory lived up to its name. The Hejaz had romance—dialing Mecca #1 rang the palace telephone in Mecca—but few resources: no universities, no industry, few roads, no motor vehicles. Most of the province was parched desert controlled by warring nomadic tribes—Bedouin—who had survived for years by raiding each other's camels and collecting tolls from pilgrimage caravans en route from Damascus. The Turks had taken even that source of income away from the Bedouin before the war, laying a railway through the desert to ease the difficulty of the pilgrimage. Now the same railroad was carrying Turkish troops and heavy weapons intended to crush the Arab revolt.

Unimpressed with both the Arab and British advisers he met upon arrival in the Hejaz, Lawrence feared that the Turks might be successful. As usual, he made no secret of his opinions. "Lawrence wants kicking, and kicking hard at that," Colonel C. E. Wilson had cabled to Cairo within days of Lawrence's arrival in the Red Sea port of Jidda. "I look on him as a bumptious young ass who spoils his undoubted knowledge of Syrian Arabs etc. by making himself out to be the only authority on war, engineering . . . ships and everything else. He put every single person's back up I've met from the Admiral down to the most junior fellow in the Red Sea." Lawrence's own assessment of the situation was not modest. "I had believed the misfortunes of the Revolt to be due mainly to faulty leadership, or rather to the lack of leadership, Arab and English," he would write in *Seven Pillars*. "So I went down to Arabia to see and consider its great men."

What Lawrence was really seeking, though, seemed to be the experiences of the great British men who had roamed the Hejaz before him. He had spent the voyage from Cairo reading the memoirs of the most famous of these, Charles Doughty, an Oxford don and doctor who had spent two years traveling among the Bedouin. Refusing all the while to conceal his Christianity, Doughty had cataloged the details of desert life even as he endured an ordeal of thirst, beatings, death threats, and abandonment. His book, *Travels in Arabia Deserta,* described a land where treacherous allies left you stranded in a "horrid sandstone desolation," and where every plate threatened to be full of poison. Lawrence, who was to use *Arabia Deserta* as both bible and military manual, saw Doughty's experiences as a kind of endurance test of English character. Doughty, he wrote later, "had experienced the test of nomadism . . . a life too hard, too empty, too denying for all but the strongest and most determined men."

But there was also another important Oxford man whom Lawrence could not help thinking about. That his name goes unmentioned in *Seven Pillars* only makes the reader consider him more closely, for no English visitor to the Hejaz could forget about Sir Richard Burton. The Irish-born Burton was a tall, dark, and handsome Oxford dropout, an imperial secret agent who spoke 35 languages and dialects and made the pilgrimage to Mecca disguised as a Muslim at the age of 33. His willingness to circumcise himself as part of his disguise, his translation of erotic literature of the East, and his elaborate descriptions of the men and women one could sleep with there had raised Victorian eyebrows and quite a few expectations.

Most of the Middle East and Asia Minor, Burton explained in an essay attached to his scandalously racy translation of *The Arabian Nights,* were in what he called the "Sotadic Zone": a geographical belt where sodomy between men was natural and popular. Burton defined the boundaries of the zone precisely—north latitude 43, north latitude 30—and claimed that while men to the north and south of this zone were "as a rule, physically incapable of performing the operation," those within had no such problems. Apparently, a little time in the right climate did wonders for one's abilities: Burton himself made a complete tour of the boy brothels of Karachi, now in Pakistan, and wrote with gusto about sex between men in other regions. In Persia, he noted, boys were prepared for sex with men by diets, baths, and hair removers. In Syria, even religious visitors to the mosques enjoyed a little homosexual romp. The caravans of Afghani traders included "traveling wives"—boys in women's clothing—and in Egypt, European influence had made the

"He was a man of moods, flickering between glory and despair. . . . Appetite and physical weakness were mated in him, with the spur of courage. His personal charm, his imprudence, the pathetic hint of frailty as the sole reserve of this proud character made him the idol of his followers." So wrote Lawrence in *Seven Pillars of Wisdom* about Prince Feisal.

upper classes shyer, but no different: "they are as vicious as ever, but they do not care for displaying their vices to the eyes of mocking strangers."

It is between these two desert adventurers that Lawrence would pitch his literary camp. *Seven Pillars* is filled with Doughty's love of endurance and Burton's delight in a sexuality, or more particularly, homosexuality, cleansed of Western complications. Like Doughty, Lawrence endured without pretending to be a Muslim or an Arab. Like Burton, Lawrence's theories and descriptions seemed to reveal as much about the unconscious of the writer as about the natives he supposedly described. "The desert Arab found no joy like the joy of voluntarily holding back," wrote Lawrence, in a line that evoked his Oxford days as much as it did the desert. Or later, "The strength of the Arabs was the strength of men geographically beyond temptation." Was it really the Arabs Lawrence was talking about? Or was it some ideal version of himself?

Being geographically beyond temptation—off the map of pleasure and guilt—is the fantasy that drives the narrative of Lawrence's time in the desert. It is a fantasy of questionable morality: it is probably no coincidence that Lawrence's guilt-free zone, like Burton's, fell in a place where he felt economically and politically dominant. But look again at young Lawrence—or any of the thousands of gays and lesbians who leave their small hometowns for big urban centers today—and you may also sympathize with his fantasy of freedom. The reality is that Lawrence's Oxford fellows were critical of his poverty, his parentage, and his sexuality. The cities of the Middle East, too, were full of European agents and sophisticated Arabs, all using whatever means and mockery they could to play one foreign representative against another. No wonder Lawrence had left his companion Storrs at the coast and continued on into the desert to find his Arab prince. From his arrival in Arabia until the end of the war, young Captain Lawrence—hanger-on and homosexual—had to work for his place in the pleasure zone.

Now, in the desert camp of Feisal, as the burning blue eyes of the English officer first met the dark eyes of the Arab prince, Lawrence began to see new possibilities. Here was a sharif—a direct descendant of the prophet Muhammad—whose heritage was everything Lawrence's was not. Here was a man whose family had ruled the Hejaz for hundreds of years, a man who had been raised in the court at Constantinople, yet was also at home in the ways of the desert. Here, wrote Lawrence in *Seven Pillars,* was the "prophet" he had been seeking, a "master-spirit" able to weld the warring Bedouin tribes into a united force.

But not, Lawrence noted with some satisfaction, without British help. He had seen Feisal's troops lying "like lizards" among the rocks as he rode up: the men were tough, but they were tired. The Turks, with their long-range guns, had scattered Arab camel raiders and trained infantry alike. And the tribes who sat around the winking campfires of the oasis read like a list of the great feuding families of the Hejaz, sheikhs who had set aside their rivalries to join Feisal's effort and his payroll. Their loyalty was likely to last only as long as the money did, and the money, Feisal confessed to Lawrence, was quickly running out. The heavy chest in Feisal's tent, which his slaves struggled so conspicuously to move, was filled with stones, not gold.

Lawrence was to be the British heart inside that Arab chest, the supplier of gold and arms. Walking around the camp, gauging the loyalty of the Bedouin, Lawrence saw the possibility of a movement that transcended tribal feuds. Hussein's family would be the leaders and the British the power. Together they could fight their way up to Syria. Feisal could be a king, Lawrence his Merlin.

All this, of course, depended on whether Lawrence could make the case in Cairo. He departed immediately. A hundred thousand pounds (about a million dollars) would be the amount that "one may perhaps suggest for the Hejaz monthly expenses," he wrote in an intelligence bulletin in December 1916. Guns, too, needed to be sent. A French suggestion that Allied forces be sent to lead the Arab effort Lawrence opposed with his usual anti-French vigor. He saw no reason to give the French more influence in the region and believed that what the Bedouin rebels lacked in terms of conventional military training they would make up for in mobility and fervor. "The Hejaz war is one of dervishes against regular troops, and we are on the side of the dervishes," Lawrence argued. "Our text books do not apply to its conditions at all." That is precisely what Lawrence loved most about this endeavor—that the books neither applied to the Arab revolt nor to him while he was in it.

His superiors were swayed. More guns, explosives, and money were to be sent to the Hejaz. A wireless radio, too, would be sent. And until a more suitable officer could be found, Lawrence would travel back to Feisal with them.

Al-sabr jamil—patience is beautiful—says an Arabic proverb. Westerners often look to proverbs to explain the East, as if the sayings somehow mean more there than our own proverbs do at home. But it is certainly true that patience—never a noticeable part of Lawrence's personality in Egypt—became his mode of operation as he sat in Feisal's tent. Watching as Feisal rallied other tribal leaders to the fight, Lawrence realized he was learning from a master. Even after Turkish troops drove down the middle of his camp, sending camels and men roaring away in fear, Feisal did not lose his calm.

During the day, in the tradition of the Bedouin, men lined up for an audience with Feisal—all who wished one were received. At sunset, Lawrence watched Feisal and the other leaders pray, cupping their hands in front of their faces as they recited the words and bowing down in the direction of Mecca. At night, sheikhs would come in for pleasure: the recitation of poetry and the singing of war songs. Listening quietly, always deferring, Lawrence learned the history of the tribes: who had fought with whom, who was related to whom, who was weak and who was powerful. Later, this knowledge would be crucial to his plan to build a "ladder of tribes" that would carry the Arab revolt all the way from the Hejaz to Damascus.

But first, with the ease of silk slipping over skin, the most famous piece of Lawrence's strategy fell into place: Feisal asked Lawrence to put on native dress. The robes he offered were the lavish wedding garments of a Meccan prince: all white, with a gold dagger and belt. Lawrence strolled alone through the palm gardens in the outfit, testing the freedom of the skirt, hefting the dagger, enjoying the coolness of the silk robes against his skin. "His great aunt had sent them from Mecca (was it a hint)?" Lawrence wondered in *Seven Pillars.* Indeed it was, but a hint to whom? To Lawrence, who was feeling more and more wedded to Feisal and to his cause? To the reader, whom Lawrence had already tantalized with descriptions of "the exquisite bodies" of the "too beautiful" camel soldiers? Or to the other British officers, many of whom openly disdained both Arab clothes and what they felt were the good-for-nothing military tactics of the tribesmen themselves?

Feisal rides with his personal bodyguard. "Feisal seemed to govern his men unconsciously: hardly to know how he stamped his mind on them, hardly to care whether they obeyed," wrote Lawrence.

Lawrence would wear his Arab wedding outfit through much of the war, in meetings with generals and privates alike. For some, like fellow Englishman Colonel Pierce Joyce, Lawrence's new robes framed a power that he had never noticed: "His appearance was such a contrast to the untidy lieutenant I'd met at Port Sudan, that one suddenly became aware of contact with a very unusual personality . . . indistinguishable from any of the nobles of the royal house of Hussein seated around us." Others, like Colonel Richard Meinertzhagen, who met Lawrence in Beersheba in 1918, found in Lawrence's costume something suspiciously alluring: "As I was working in my tent . . . in walked an Arab boy, dressed in spotless white, white headdress and a golden circlet; for the moment I thought the boy was somebody's pleasure boy, but it soon dawned on me that he must be Lawrence whom I knew to be in camp. I just stared in silence at the very beautiful apparition. . . . He then said in a soft voice, 'I am Lawrence, Dalmeny sent me over to see you.' I said [are you a] 'boy or girl?' He smiled and blushed, saying 'boy.'"

In the early days of the Arab rebellion, Lawrence lived in the Red Sea city of Yenbo, in the house on the right.

For Lawrence himself, Arab clothes were a two-way disguise, a veil behind which he could live out his double life. To his British colleagues he presented himself as the undercover agent, using his new clothes to manipulate the Arabs into doing what was necessary for the British plan: "If you wear Arab things at all, go the whole way. Leave your English friends and customs on the coast. . . . It is possible, starting thus level with them, for Europeans to beat the Arabs at their own game," he advised in the manual he wrote on the handling of the Bedouin. But in his more personal reflections, his robes seemed to help him slip out of the confines of British identity and into the all-consuming, all-male Arab struggle. "We were fond together, because of the sweep of the open places, the taste of wide winds, the sunlight and the hopes in which we worked," Lawrence wrote in *Seven Pillars*. Describing those first days with Feisal, hanging on his every word, Lawrence's language might in England have been taken for a love poem: "I learned much of the men and parties in the Hejaz from his lips."

The desert traditions that so warmed Lawrence's heart, though, could only have been chilling to the British command. The untrained Bedouin warriors seemed to be helpless against the Turks—returning to the coastal city of Yenbo (today's Yanbu' al Bahr) in December 1916 to rally reinforcements, Lawrence had hardly arrived before learning that Feisal and his brother Zeid had been driven by the Turks back from the interior again. From the city gates, Lawrence photographed the Arabs' beaten forces as they straggled in, foot soldiers first, then sheikhs on horseback, and a ragged line of camels behind. The Turks, with other, anti-British Bedouin as guides, were hot on their trail. "Our war," Lawrence wrote, "seemed entering its last act."

If Lawrence was to be Merlin for his future king, he had to work some British magic. Within hours, there were five British warships moored in Yenbo harbor, their big guns and searchlights trained on the plains over which the enemy would have to come. Other British officers organized the townspeople to throw up ramparts of dirt to serve as fortress walls. The Arabs took up positions on the walls. And the Turks, creeping down to stamp out the last of Feisal's army, turned back in fear.

The Turks would yield again a few weeks later, and a few hundred miles north, at the port of Wejh (called Al Wajh today). Once again, the British would provide the force, and Feisal would serve as the Arab figurehead. Lawrence rode with Feisal, thrilling at the sight of the lines of tribesmen waving banners and palm fronds behind them and the sound of ten thousand voices raised in throaty war songs. The nomads killed lizards and rabbits with sticks as they rode, and British warships sent out supplies to help them make it through parts of the desert so bare that there were not even stewed thorn buds or locusts to eat. When the Bedouin arrived at Wejh, British ships had already taken the town, and the camelhair tents of the Arab victors soon stretched for miles next to the khaki shelters of the British Command. Lawrence made a point of walking barefoot along the scorching coral paths that joined the two camps, toughening his feet, and his mind, for the battles to come.

But the most decisive battles for control of the Middle East, Lawrence would discover, were being fought at conference tables in Europe. Even as Lawrence and Feisal were promising independence to all Arabs who joined them, other British were plotting it away. By the terms of a secret treaty signed by representatives of the government of Britain and France in early 1916, known as the Sykes-Picot Agreement, those two allies had agreed to divide Syria and Mesopotamia between them after the war. The French were anxious to get a head start: Colonel Edouard Bremond of their army called on Lawrence to propose landing a joint British-French force at Aqaba, the port city at the head of the gulf of the same name, which separates the Sinai and Arabian peninsulas. (Al 'Aqabah, as it is known today, lies at the southwesternmost extreme of the present-day nation of Jordan.) Meanwhile, the officers of the British Command were urging Feisal and his brothers to return south to face down the 16,000 Turks at Medina. They were worried that the Turks might give up on the Hejaz altogether and move those troops to join with their forces fighting the British in Palestine.

Lawrence had yet to kill a man in battle, but he disagreed with all his Allied superiors. Why allow the French any foothold in Syria at all? And why send Bedouin forces to confront the better-trained Turks at Medina? Lawrence believed the Arabs could do more damage to the Turks

Lawrence of Arabia on camelback: Early on in *Seven Pillars of Wisdom,* he confessed to not being "a skilled rider," but some of the journeys he completed belie that statement.

as an anxiety, an unpredictable nuisance, a guerrilla force that materialized out of the desert, struck, and then disappeared again. Lawrence had learned from his time in Feisal's tents that tribesmen could cross terrain the Allies thought impenetrable. To the Bedouin, a camel was a roving supply station: its dung was fuel; its milk, drink; its urine, shampoo. Riders could double up when necessary and kill their spare camels for meat. A band of warriors could range a thousand miles without having to resupply. The port of Aqaba and the fifty miles of mountains behind it could be taken, Lawrence thought, as he studied the map for oases at which a raiding party could water. But not by a French or British naval force. It would be taken by the Arabs themselves.

Thirty-five riders, each with a sack of flour slung on his saddle, were in the raiding party that left Wejh the morning of May 9, 1917. Six pack camels carried explosives, guns, and British gold. Only the fastest camels and the toughest riders could hope to make the trip. Feisal, sending his trusted friend Sharif Nasir from Medina in his stead, stayed behind.

The ranking British officers, tied to their warships and their plan to smash Medina, stayed behind. But Lawrence went, astride a splendid racing camel that Feisal had given him. Cairo intelligence would have scoffed at the notion of their youngest liaison officer and a small party of tribesmen capturing one of the most important ports in the Red Sea—had they known about it. But Lawrence, certain that permission would be denied him, had not asked for any.

The men set out first for the grazing pastures of the Howeitat, the tribe commanded by the legendary Auda Abu Tayi, who rode at the head of the raiding party. The tall, bearded Sheikh Auda was like a character out of the legends of King Arthur, a volume of which Lawrence carried in his saddlebag. It was Auda who had convinced Lawrence that Aqaba was takeable. He had been married 28 times and wounded 13. He had killed 75 men in battle by his own hand, not including Turks. His right arm was stiff from a wound, his long black hair was streaked with white, he spoke of himself always in the third person, and his cry in battle—"Dogs, do you not know Auda!"—had been enough to

Flying the flag of the Arab rebellion, Lawrence leads the Bedouin into battle.

reduce whole villages to surrender. At the slightest opportunity he burst into poetry and song. Lawrence and the others followed his deep voice at night as they wound their way to the north through the cliffs that lay between them and the desert.

At times the track was so steep that it took two men to lead each camel. When the animals fell, according to *Seven Pillars,* the Howeitat pulled the mounts' heads toward their saddles, drove a dagger into their necks, and shared out the meat. At other times, the path wound through deep gorges of red sandstone or through mazes of razor-sharp lava. Through it all Auda led steadily, gauging his way by a hoofprint or a camel dropping, shouting out the names of the rock formations and valleys to Lawrence, who was busily scribbling down maps and military notes. Lawrence's extraordinary memory recorded everything: sand hard enough for armored cars to pass over, wells where troops might water, patches of brush where camels, with their long lips, could graze without fear of thorns.

The journey's importance to Lawrence, however, was more spiritual than strategic. In *Seven Pillars,* he describes how the camels crossed for hours over vast stretches of mud that had been baked by the sun until it was as smooth as paper or sank to their knees in sand as sticky as glue. Occasionally a few men dismounted, crawling on their hands and knees up a sand dune to spy on the railroad and check for Turkish patrols. When the raiders finally did cross the railway line they dragged down the Turkish telegraph wires with their camels, and Lawrence used some explosives to blow up the rails. Auda, who had never seen dynamite before, made up a poem of praise on the spot.

The sun seemed to beat down twice onto the journeyers—once upon their heads, and then again as it reflected off the glittering sand. The raiders' eyes streamed; their bodies ached; their camels were tortured by mange. Lawrence broke out in boils and was racked with fever, and the hot wind drove his eyelids back until his eyeballs felt bare. At first he practiced his Arabic with Auda to pass the difficult hours, replacing his Syrian dialect with the slang of the desert tribesman. Later, his tongue thick and black in his mouth and his lips cracked for lack of water, he remained silent.

Passions and tempers flared in the heat of the desert. Young men had sex with each other in the hot sand, enjoying what Lawrence called the "Eastern boy and boy affection which the segregation of women made inevitable." One pair of young lovers, Daud and Farraj, accidentally set their tent on fire and, fearing a beating, asked Lawrence to beg their captain for lenience. The best Lawrence could negotiate was for both youths to share the punishment. Later both came to him, saluted, and asked to be his servants. Lawrence resisted—he had no need for servants. But Farraj's "innocent, smooth face and swimming eyes," and the fact that both boys looked "so young and clean," won him over. The boys would stay with Lawrence through many battles, packing his bags, dressing his camel's mange with butter, making his coffee, and keeping up a constant stream of practical jokes. Lawrence saw their "only sin as joyfulness" and admired their "instinctive understanding with each other against the demands of the world."

The demands of the British world, and its ideas of sin, must have seemed more and more abstract to Lawrence. What did an illegitimate birth mean in the barren desert, where all birth seemed impossible? Here, away from the buildings and the British, in the sand and "virile heat," even homosexuality seemed clean and pure, and Lawrence seemed to revel in it. "We had no shut places to be alone in, no thick clothes to hide our nature," he wrote exultantly on the second page of *Seven Pillars,* as if not wanting to wait a moment for the reader to understand this important point:

> Our youths began indifferently to slake one another's few needs in their own clean bodies—a cold convenience that . . . seemed sexless, and even pure. Later some began to justify this sterile process, and swore that friends quivering together in the yielding sand with intimate hot limbs in supreme embrace, found there hidden in the darkness a sensual co-efficient of the mental passion which was welding our souls and spirits in one flaming effort.

Our youth. *Our* souls and spirits. Lawrence played his role as British agent for the commanders in Cairo, but in the desert he felt he was one with the Arab cause. He quenched his thirst like the Bedouin—drinking till vomiting at each well, and then going dry to the next. He ate like the Bedouin, scavenging ostrich eggs or choking down cakes of flour and water baked in the campfire. He rode as hard and as long as the others, even turning his exhausted camel back into the blazing desert to find one of the men, Gasim, who had dropped off his saddle. Auda was enraged, claiming that the man's life was not worth the price of a camel. But Lawrence found Gasim, black mouth open and gasping under the desert sun, and brought him back.

In this terrain, where pain and bravery overlapped, Lawrence felt in his element. A windstorm blew up, sweeping a wall of sand into the raiders' faces. The Bedouin pulled their cloaks over their faces, preferring the stifling heat to the cuts caused by the thousand stinging particles of sand. Lawrence preferred to face the storm directly, "challenging its strength," as the sand needles opened his skin. At night, resting, the raiders faced different dangers. At one camp, a sniper's rifle cracked out, and one unlucky victim pitched forward into the campfire. Several died in the three weeks it took the raiders to reach Wadi Sirhan, the chain of oases where Auda's own flocks were grazing. But miraculously, Lawrence was alive, the raiding party's camels were intact, and they still had their explosives.

Feasting on roasted mutton and rice in Wadi Sirhan, the raiders restrategized. Aqaba and the Turks lay to the northwest—only with the cooperation of local tribesmen, Auda assured them, could they hope to reach their target. Nuri Shaalan, the sheikh in whose valley they now rested, was an essential ally, and Auda was dispatched with gold to win his support. Lawrence moved up the Wadi to recruit other Howeitat, at each camp being greeted by joyful shouts, shots fired in welcome, and gifts of food.

But for Lawrence, all was far from joyful. The complications of international politics were sullying the purity of the desert. Every night, tribesmen asked Lawrence for assurances that the British supported Arab independence. Every night Lawrence gave those assurances, well realizing that Britain's secret agreements might make them useless. His trip had wedded him to the Bedouin and awakened passions he had never known. But would loyalty to his country require him to betray his new friends in the end? "All day, deputations, fusillades, coffee, ostrich eggs,"

Sheikh Auda Abu Tayi (seated, second from right, in dark robes) convinced Lawrence that the Arabs should attempt to take the port city of Aqaba. "He saw life as a saga," Lawrence wrote. "All the events in it were significant; all personages in contact with him heroic."

Lawrence scribbled despairingly in his diary, stuffing the tiny pages into his belt to keep them safe. "Dined with Auda. Lies."

In *Seven Pillars,* even the descriptions of the desert seem to mirror Lawrence's guilt and confusion. The camp swarmed with snakes—traditional Christian phallic symbols of deceit, temptation, and betrayal. The reptiles slithered into the men's blankets at night and killed three with their poisonous bites. Farraj and Daud laughed off the danger, but Lawrence was terrified both by the reptiles and by his growing doubt. "I've decided to go off alone to Damascus, hoping to get killed on the way. . . . We're calling on them to fight for us on a lie and I can't stand it," he scribbled in a note to Cairo that he had no way to send. Then, mounting his camel, he rode off on a suicide mission to scout out Turkish territory. *Seven Pillars* does not mention the trip, but Lowell Thomas would later claim that Lawrence had disguised himself as a woman to get past enemy lines, putting on a long dress and pulling a heavy veil over his face to slip past the Turkish sentries.

Two weeks later, prepared to press forward, Lawrence returned. Auda was back too, with permission to use Wadi Sirhan as a base, and with a contingent of horsemen willing to join the fight. A breakfast of camel calf cooked in sour milk, and their growing numbers, put the men in good humor: the band of 35 had now swelled to more than 500. Shortly after their departure for Aqaba, the Bedouin received news that the Turks had sent out a party of equal number, armed with heavy artillery, to head them off.

Using local tribesmen as guides, Auda and his men surrounded the Turks as they slept in the valley of Bir El-Lissan. High on the rocks, Auda knew, the Arabs would be safe from the Turks' big guns. The two forces traded potshots all morning until Auda, with fifty men on horseback, finally tipped the balance, charging straight down the hill into the enemy camp. Sheikh Nasir, Lawrence, and the others followed on camels, the Bedouin leaning expertly to fire to the left and the right even as their mounts pitched furiously down the incline. Lawrence got off four shots with a revolver, but his fifth landed in the head of his own camel, and as the animal came crashing down, the world went dark.

The battle was over by the time Lawrence regained consciousness. Auda's horse, field glasses, and sword scabbard all had bullet holes in them, but the old Howeitat remained as indestructible as ever. The Arabs had lost only two men, but 300 Turks lay dead or dying and 160 had been taken prisoner. The Howeitat were happily plundering the Turkish supplies, stripping the uniforms off the Turkish dead to wear as trophies of victory. Lawrence found the naked, ivory-skinned Turkish soldiers beautiful in the moonlight.

Most of the other Turkish outposts on the road to Aqaba were deserted. They had been built to prepare for a naval attack, the Turks never imagining that enemy forces might come from the desert, and they had been abandoned as indefensible. On July 6, just two months after leaving Wejh, Lawrence and the others rode triumphantly into Aqaba. Lawrence took photos as he and the others, racing through a sandstorm and waving Hussein's red, green, and black banner, drove their camels knee-deep into the Red Sea surf.

CHAPTER SEVEN

FUN WITH TRAINS

"Mush Fadi," Brigadier-General Gilbert Clayton snapped at the thin, ragged Bedouin standing in sandals at the door of his Cairo office. "I'm busy." The Bedouin spoke, and the director of Cairo intelligence looked up again, his annoyance turned to surprise. It was not a Bedouin standing there at all. It was Lawrence.

Clayton and the rest of the British estabishment in Cairo went into shock as Lawrence relayed the story of his past two months. Not only had Lawrence and his band managed to take Aqaba, but within hours Lawrence and eight tribesmen had jumped on the best camels and ridden for fifty hours straight across the Sinai desert to Cairo to fetch help. There was hardly any food at all at Aqaba, and no loot to satisfy the restless tribesmen. Auda and the others were living on boiled camel meat, raw dates, and the promise held by the pieces of paper Lawrence had written out as checks for the warriors. Now Lawrence needed gold to make

Lawrence poses amid the wreckage of a train he demolished in 1917.

good on those pledges, food, and troops to make sure the 50,000 Turks at nearby Maan did not strike back.

Lawrence's Aqaba expedition was to win him a promotion to major, a medal from the king, and a place in military history. Everybody had known Lawrence was intelligent, but no one had suspected him to be a soldier. "His reputation is overpowering," Hogarth wrote to his sister from Cairo. Clayton, whose reports would refer to Lawrence's feats as "little short of marvelous," arranged immediately for money to be sent, along with supplies, from Suez. He also brought Lawrence to meet the new commander of the eastern front, recently arrived from France: General Edmund Allenby.

It must have been one of the more unusual meetings of World War I: the 56-year-old, stocky General Allenby, affectionately known as "the Bull," and the small, blond man, half his age, in a silk skirt and headdress. Lawrence arrived barefoot, no doubt enjoying the impression he was making as he spread out a map and explained that with £100,000 he could deliver eastern Syria to the Allies and cut the railway now supplying the Turks in both Palestine and the Hejaz. Allenby "looked sideways" at Lawrence the whole time, *Seven Pillars* noted, trying to make out how seriously to take the dramatics. But the performance worked. Allenby would send twice the requested sum to Lawrence over the next months. Feisal, as a recognized part of Allenby's forces, would be allowed to conduct operations outside of the Hejaz. And Aqaba, complete with warships, armored cars, and British troops, would become the supply base for the Palestine front of the British army.

By September, Lawrence and Feisal were together again, mapping out a strategy to carry the revolt north. Feisal needed to stay in Aqaba to receive tribal leaders, they decided, but small raiding parties could fan out under his flag to destroy the railroad and win recruits. Different raiders would blow up the railway in different districts, cruising on camelback much as a navy's warships patrolled the sea. Soon, Lawrence hoped, the Turks in the Hejaz desert would not be able to withdraw even if they wanted to: they would not be able to find a train to take them.

The British warship *Humber* stands guard over Aqaba in August 1917. Lawrence, who took this photo of the ship, often went on board to visit with the ship's officers and enjoy some of the amenities of home, particularly "a hot bath, and tea with civilized trappings, free from every suspicion of blown sand."

The first such raid, conducted east of Aqaba near Mudawwara, Lawrence led himself. Auda, Daud, and Farraj all went with him, as did a few British gunners. On their way to recruit more help from local Bedouin, the band rode through Wadi Rumm, which even the unsentimental Howeitat had told Lawrence was beautiful. Arabs and Englishmen alike were awed to silence by the thousand-foot-high red walls of rock stretching out before them, and the waterfall that crashed from 300 feet above onto the canyon floor. "[W]ithin the walls a squadron of airplanes could have wheeled in formation," Lawrence marveled in *Seven Pillars*. "Landscapes, in childhood's dream, were so vast and silent."

All were silent again at the bridge near Mudawwara, where they watched a train roll toward the mine Lawrence had laid for it. He had spent five hours putting the explosives in place, using rocks and dirt to conceal them, and finally taking his cloak and sweeping away any marks he had left in the sand. Now, high on the hillside, one of Feisal's slaves waited anxiously for the signal to depress the plunger and send the bridge sky-high. A detachment of raiders was hidden behind a spur of rock, their rifles at the ready. The British gunners, shells loaded, were in position. The train shrieked around the corner—two locomotives, ten boxcars full of Turkish soldiers, and many baggage cars behind. As the second engine passed over the mine, Lawrence raised his arm, Feisal's slave pushed his downward, and the scene exploded into madness.

Seven Pillars describes the chaos: the deafening blast, the Turks pouring out of the overturned cars and opening fire, and the British gunners killing them by the dozen. Bedouin anxious for loot ripped open the boxcars, screaming and firing at the passengers and at each other and staggering backward with huge bales of carpets, kettles, blankets, and clothes. Tribesmen new to the fight even tried to snatch the clothes and dagger off Lawrence himself, their judgment blurred in the frenzy. Screaming passengers clutched at Lawrence, too, though he kicked them away with his bare feet. Turks would be there to help them soon enough—through his binoculars, Lawrence had seen them on their way from Mudawwara station. By the time the enemy arrived, however, Lawrence and his men had disappeared, making off with ninety military prisoners, enough booty to keep each tribesman set for a year, and only one casualty.

Nothing succeeds like success: Feisal's tent at Aqaba was soon full of tribal leaders anxious to take part in similar expeditions. And news spread across Syria about "El-Aurans," the train-wrecking Englishman who could spring into the saddle while the camel was still moving. "Send us a 'lurens' and we will blow up a train with it!" the sheikh of the Bani Atiyeh tribe wrote Feisal. "Welcome, Aurans, harbinger of action!" others called as the Englishman rode up, bare feet pressed against the camel's neck like a native, his saddlebags full of English gold and explosives. The British demolition experts who worked with Lawrence later were more balanced in their praise. Lawrence, it seemed, liked to use more explosive than necessary for a job.

"Tulips," Lawrence called the mines he planted under the rails, naming them for the explosions that blossomed from the sandy soil. Over the next four months, Lawrence and the Aqaba team he trained would destroy 17 trains. Soon Syrian passengers were deciding not to travel or paying extra for seats farthest away from the locomotive. In a different way, Lawrence, too, was distancing himself from the engines of modern life—he was still staying off the map, blowing up the guidelines, and hiding behind a veil of noise and smoke. To shield himself further from fellow Englishmen, Lawrence added another layer of protection: contradiction. To some friends, he would insist that he was having a marvelous time; to others, he would say that the work was a "nightmare" that he longed to have end.

However mysterious Lawrence's personality, though, the British command was coming to see the value of his work quite clearly. In the fall of 1917, Allenby included Lawrence in his plan for a major offensive on the Palestine front. At precisely the moment that the British drove

Lawrence took this photograph of the Turks repairing the Hejaz railway. "We were able, till the end of the war, to descend upon the railway when and where we pleased, and effect the damage we wished, without great difficulty," he wrote.

through the Turkish line at Beersheba, Lawrence was to slip behind enemy lines and blow up a bridge, crippling the Turkish ability to resupply. It was a dangerous trip, but it was also the first time that Allenby had counted on Lawrence and his raiders so directly, and he could not refuse.

Lawrence would make the trip with two leaders new to him: Abdel Kader, sheikh of the villages that stood near their destination, and Sharif Ali ibn El Hussein, sheikh of the Harith tribe. A company of Indian machine gunners were to participate as well, as were Farraj and Daud, though on the morning of departure the two boys were nowhere to be found. Lawrence finally located them—in jail! The governor of Aqaba's prize racing camel had turned up with her head and legs dyed all different colors, and Farraj and Daud had literally been caught red-handed.

But even the newly freed pranksters could not make this trip lighthearted. The Indians, unused to camel riding, were slow; Abdel Kader was argumentative. Auda and his Howeitat, fearing there would be little loot and distrustful of Abdel Kader, declined to join the raid at all. The Bani Serahin, a tribe whose camels grazed nearer the target, were even more discouraging. Turks had just filled the woods, they told Lawrence, and it was unlikely that a raiding party could slip through undetected.

In *Seven Pillars,* Lawrence described his desperate state. The English guns firing on Beersheba were already audible, and now Lawrence began his own assault. He preached to the Serahin gathered round the camp fire, his Arabic ringing out full in the night. To fight with sure success was no honor at all, Lawrence exhorted the Serahin, but to fight with sure defeat was one of the most noble endeavors. The only real victory came from flying in the face of the unconquerable, going "down into death fighting and crying for failure itself." Lawrence cajoled and thundered until the fire spread from him to all who listened, and the reluctance of the Serahin warriors was replaced by eagerness. The next day, even those without rifles picked up stones and joined the raiding party. And Abdel Kader disappeared, gone to warn the Turks of Lawrence's intentions.

The raiders moved on quickly, beating the camels with sticks, trying to reach their target before Abdel Kader reached his. Rain fell heavily, and soon so did the camels, going down in the mud of the fields over which the raiders crossed. Frightened tribesmen began to quarrel, feign illness, and threaten violence against each other: Lawrence and Ali had all they could do to keep peace. It was near dawn before the band, wet and miserable, took their positions within sight of their objective: the bridge and the tents of the Turkish sentries assigned to guard it.

This time, however, it was the Turks who triumphed. One of Lawrence's men dropped a rifle, and guards poured out of the tent and opened fire. Afraid the blasting gelatin would explode, Lawrence's porters threw it down a ravine and ran for cover. Lawrence sat there, helpless in the rain and darkness, watching as the entire operation was ruined. The next week, while mining a train to get food, he and the others would score a small victory in killing Javed Pasha, commander of the Turkish Eighth Army Corps, as he hurried down to defend Jerusalem against Allenby. But five different bullets would graze Lawrence in that raid, some deeply. Their sting, and the pain of failure, haunted him.

Lawrence was also experiencing a different kind of haunting in the form of Sharif Ali, the Harith sheikh from Mecca. "No one could see him without the desire to see him again, especially when he smiled," Lawrence wrote in *Seven Pillars*. Ali always dressed all in black or all in white, and even watching as his "white feet flashed beneath . . . his cashmere robes" was enough to launch Lawrence into a discussion of "physical perfection." Despite his small size, Lawrence was no weakling—he could hold the end of a rifle and raise the gun over his head without bending his arm—but Ali could rise from a kneeling position with a man standing on each of his open palms, and he could outrun a camel for a mile and a half in bare feet. "I am Harith," was the battle cry that broke out of Ali in a fight, his huge black eyes flashing. His laugh, Lawrence wrote, made "the youth, boyish or girlish in him . . . break through his night like sunrise." Yet Ali also had a constant seriousness and an "unwilling detachment."

Lawrence (at extreme right, wearing wristwatch) confers with Feisal (crouching, next to him) and other Bedouin at an undisclosed location.

Strength, irrepressible laughter at once boyish and girlish, an unwilling detachment—once again, Lawrence had found himself in his description of an Arab. Even the setting in which he was to spend much of his time with Ali—the deserted castle of Azraq, which the two made their northern base—seemed to have come from a T. E. Lawrence fantasy. Built by early shepherd kings, the stone castle with six towers and beautiful pools was filled, in Lawrence's words, with "memories of wandering poets, champions, lost kingdoms." Ali and his men took one tower, covering the stone rafters with palm leaves to keep out the incessant rain; Lawrence and his men slept in another.

There, as the cold winter descended, Lawrence and Ali ruled as kings. A sentry was posted at the huge stone door, and a hall prepared to receive the guests that came to hear of Feisal and the Arab armies. Merchants from Damascus brought news—the Turks had placed a price on the heads of Lawrence and Ali both—as well as presents of nuts, carpets, and head cloths. In return, Lawrence and Ali offered cotton and sugar from Aqaba, goods in scarce supply outside the port. At night, all would gather around a huge fire on the floor of either Lawrence's or Ali's room, trading stories. Often the castle would echo with a strange, animal howling. The Bedouin said that the ghosts of the dogs of the Bani Hillal, the builders of the fort, still roamed the six towers in search of their masters.

When the rain came down in earnest, streaming through the make-shift palm-leaf roof, Lawrence and Ali and their men were left alone. They built platforms of branches to keep off the wet floor and huddled together under sheepskins while mist drifted in through the windows. "Past and future flowed over us like an uneddying river," Lawrence wrote in *Seven Pillars*. "We dreamed ourselves into the spirit of the place; sieges and feasting, raids, murders, love-singing in the night."

What dreams was Lawrence having as he lay there thinking of the Arabs and the English, the two allies battling for his heart? Could he hear in the howls of the ghost-dogs some reflection of his own anguished search for a master, some cry that sounded some of his own animal longings? Was it thoughts of Allenby or Ali that made Lawrence toss in his sheepskins, and finally, to leave the castle for the cold, wet countryside? *Seven Pillars* does not say. It tells us only that Lawrence, dressed in a local boy's ragged clothing, set out in the cold November weather to scout out the valley of the Hauran and the Turkish stronghold of Deraa. It was to be a short trip, only a few days. Lawrence, by his own account, would return from it changed forever.

CHAPTER EIGHT

RAPE AT DERAA

What is fact and what is fantasy? That question swirls like a sandstorm around the story you are reading now, and around the story of the Arab revolt as a whole. *Seven Pillars of Wisdom,* from which much of what we know about Lawrence is taken, was written years after the events it describes, leaving Lawrence plenty of time to smooth away uncomfortable facts as carefully as he wiped away the traces of the mines he laid under the railroad. Biographers have combed over Lawrence's accounts, searching for the truth. In some accounts, like Lowell Thomas's, Lawrence's deeds grew greater even as he himself grew smaller: Lawrence became a five-foot-five White God, ruling among a primitive people, the only British soldier allowed to go beyond Aqaba to the Syrian front. In others, such as the biography written by a shell-shocked and embittered World War I veteran, Richard Aldington, Lawrence was portrayed as a coward who went to the desert to avoid the front, a self-promoter who lied about everything from the numbers of books he had read to the numbers of trains he had wrecked.

The person in this photograph is often said to be Lawrence, disguised as a woman for a foray behind enemy lines. Although the picture's authenticity has been questioned, Lawrence certainly was known to disguise himself for reconnaissance missions.

The "truth" is clouded further by Lawrence's love of rewriting his own history. "I find that my fifth writing . . . of a sentence makes it more shapely, pithier, stranger than it was," Lawrence once wrote. "Without that twist of strangeness no one would feel an individuality, a differentness, behind the phrase." For all his self-denial, Lawrence was never above the pleasure of enhancing his own role—friends and family would hear detailed stories, often quite unlikely, of how he survived failed assassination attempts, arranged the surrender of Turkish garrisons, or spent a month in a British Q-boat. Lawrence himself provided Lowell Thomas with much of the information contained in his book and then condemned Thomas's biography as a vulgar assortment of "red hot lies." Even the revelations of *Seven Pillars* were manipulated and controlled by Lawrence for maximum effect. He printed one run of the book privately, at the *Oxford Times,* to give to his colleagues and friends. Another version of *Seven Pillars,* with elaborate illustrations, was printed in a private edition for two hundred subscribers. Still a third version was a mass-market best-seller published under the title *Revolt in the Desert.* Each text was distinct, edited to reveal different things to a different audience.

And to add to the mystery, that audience—like the audience for the many Lawrence biographies that were to follow—was Western. No matter how deep or probing their enquiries, most of the biographies written about Lawrence for the forty years after the Arab revolt left unquestioned the central premise of Lawrence's fantasy: that a European was the only one who could have made it happen. Researchers compared Lawrence's reports to those of his European colleagues, took a magnifying glass to scribbled notes found in the British archives, scrutinized his bookshelves after his death. But few authors—and those not until the 1960s, when Auda and Feisal and Nasir and the others who fought alongside Lawrence were dead—ever went to the Middle East to do their research there. The desert, and the Arabs, were left silent.

The Palestinian critic Edward Said has identified this Eastern silence as a necessary hallmark of what he calls the tradition of the "Orientalists"—the Western scholar-experts whose work helped Europeans understand, and dominate, the East. It was the Orientalists who, entering "timeless" settings, were always claiming to bring them alive. In Lawrence's life, this process of bringing the ageless to life is a unifying theme, the quality that makes sense of his transformation from archaeologist to movement-maker. In Arabia, just as at Carchemish, Lawrence was excavating something hidden, raising it to modern consciousness, and in so doing, making it his own. Lawrence's account of his tribal raids, and his destruction of the railway that is the mark of an encroaching modernity, reinforce that fantasy. *Seven Pillars'* lavishly detailed landscapes include remarkably few features of the modern world. Airplanes appear rarely; visits to the telegraph office are not noted; the wireless radio is unmentioned. Absent, too, are the complexities of the Arab position. Lawrence has all the worries and ambivalences, the concerns for pragmatics, and the strategies. The Arabs are "children" who can be "swung on an idea like a cord," see things in "black and white," and are "removed from doubt, our modern crown of thorns."

Arab historians and Western biographers such as John Mack, who finally went to interview the Arabs, found a more complicated story. Some remembered Lawrence as "a prince," but others saw him as "a servant" of Feisal's. Even Lawrence's most adoring biographers have had to acknowledge that Feisal and Hussein were constantly assessing and reassessing their options, talking with the Turks as well as the British, wondering how they could best advance their interests against those of other, competing families in Arabia. The tiny mention *Seven Pillars* makes of the most notable of these rivals, Ibn Saud, shows how much more Lawrence said about the way he wanted affairs in the Hejaz to be than about the way they were. Within 10 years of the war, Ibn Saud, with his own Arabic-speaking, robe-wearing British adviser, H. St. John Philby, would attack and defeat Hussein, creating what is today the Kingdom of Saudi Arabia.

Nor do many Arabs remember the details of the revolt in quite the same way as Lawrence. Arab biographer Suleiman Mousa claims that it was Feisal and Auda, and not Lawrence, who came up with the idea of attacking Aqaba. And while the heroics of the battles Lawrence described were real, so were the economics that Lawrence glosses over.

"I remember Lawrence—he was the one with the money," one Bedouin told a researcher writing on Saudi Arabia. *Seven Pillars* mentions "Aurans" and "El Aurans," but it does not mention Lawrence's other nickname among the Arabs: Abu Khayall, or "Father of the Horseman," which he received for distributing so many gold coins embossed with a horseman on one side.

But then, Lawrence never pretended to record the simple truth, and his English audience certainly was not interested in hearing it. As it was, critic Herbert Read found *Seven Pillars* too self-questioning to qualify Lawrence for heroism. And Lawrence was open about the fact that *Seven Pillars* was as much meditation as memoir. "The manner is greater than the matter, so far as modern history is concerned," he wrote later. "The documents are liars." He also spoke of wanting to write a volume to join what he called the three "titanic" works of fiction: *The Brothers Karamazov,* by the 19th-century Russian novelist Fyodor Dostoevsky; *Thus Spake Zarathustra,* by the 19th-century German philosopher Friedrich Nietzsche; and *Moby Dick,* by the 19th-century American novelist Herman Melville.

There is no more greatly debated chapter in *Seven Pillars,* no time when Lawrence and his biographers seem more to blend fact and fiction, than in the story of his trip from the castle of Azraq to Deraa. There, Lawrence claims, he was beaten and raped by a Turkish official, Hajim Bey, and his staff. Some biographers insist the incident never happened; others claim it happened elsewhere; still others say that it was the moment at which Lawrence was permanently changed. The town of Deraa, where the spurs of the Hejaz railway converged, was of relative strategic importance, but in *Seven Pillars* Deraa's psychological importance transcends any specifics. What did Lawrence discover there? And what truths, in relaying the story of his rape, did he tell?

The story, according to Lawrence, began shortly after he had left Sharif Ali in the Azraq castle and entered Deraa disguised in native clothing. There, walking down the street, a Turkish sergeant arrested him. "The Bey wants you," the officer said, referring to Deraa's governor. Then the sergeant led Lawrence into a guardroom, where he was made to give up his belt and knife and wash himself carefully.

Lawrence in the black robes and headdress that Ali gave him.

Not long after dark, three men came to lead him to the bedroom of Hajim Bey.

As Lawrence recalls in *Seven Pillars,* the bey was a bulky, fair-skinned man, sweating and trembling: "He began to fawn on me, saying how white and fresh I was, how fine my hands and feet, and how he would let me off drills and duties . . . even pay me wages, if I would love him." When Lawrence resisted, the bey "sharply ordered me to take off my drawers," then called for a sentry to hold Lawrence's arms while he tore off the British officer's clothes. When the bey pawed his naked body, Lawrence kneed him in the groin and was promptly restrained by more guards.

Once Lawrence had been rendered helpless, the bey came back for more. "He leaned forward, fixed his teeth in my neck and bit till the blood came. Then he kissed me. Afterward he drew one of the men's bayonets . . . pulled up a fold of the flesh over my ribs, [and] worked the point through . . . I winced, while the blood wavered down my side. He looked pleased and dabbled it over my stomach with his fingertips."

Sensing Lawrence's resistance, the bey spoke. "You must understand that I know: and it will be easier if you do as I wish." Lawrence stared at him, and the bey stared back, "while the men who felt an inner meaning beyond their experience, shifted uncomfortably." Then, according to *Seven Pillars,* Lawrence threw his chin up and out in the Arab sign for "No!" and the bey ordered the guards to take him out and teach him "everything."

Everything, it seemed, meant everything humiliating. The men threw Lawrence face down on a guard bench, two kneeling on his ankles and two holding his wrists and neck against the wood. The corporal, the youngest and handsomest of the group, ran downstairs to fetch a Circassian whip, "a thong of supple black hide, rounded and tapering from the thickness of a thumb at the grip (which was wrapped in silver) down to a hard point finer than a pencil." The "flaming wire" wrapped around Lawrence's body until he cried. After the corporal stopped whipping Lawrence, another man began. The ordeal went on and on, and Lawrence remembered that the men would "squabble for the next turn, ease themselves, and play unspeakably with me." Each time a new man took up the whip he would pull Lawrence's head back to show him the mark of the lash on his back, the "hard white ridge, like a railway, darkening slowly into crimson."

When the awful punishment was nearly over, Lawrence remembered lying on the ground, smiling idly at the corporal. "A delicious warmth, probably sexual, was swelling through me," he recalled, and in response the man "flung up his arm and hacked with the full length of his whip into my groin." After that, Lawrence wrote, two men pulled his legs apart, and a third man "rode me astride." When he was at last brought back, covered in blood and vomit, the bey rejected him as "too torn," and he was thrown into a supply room. From there, taking some clothes hanging on the hook in the next room, Lawrence escaped through an unlocked door.

There is no way to know if this awful brutality ever happened, though it is certainly possible. Male-male rape, less talked about than male-female rape, is not at all uncommon in prisons, military settings, or even schools and homes. Young gay men are often the victims of rape by older men, their siblings, or their peers. In the United States, according to a 1985 Bureau of Justice report, an estimated 120,000 cases of male-male rape occurred between 1975 and 1985, making men more than eight percent of all rape victims in that period.

But did it happen to Lawrence? Colonel Richard Meinertzhagen, who stayed in the same hotel as Lawrence during the Paris peace talks after the war, claims to have seen welts on Lawrence's back when Lawrence was in the bathtub. To him, and to others, including Lawrence's friends Charlotte Shaw and E. M. Forster, Lawrence mentioned various versions of the rape at Deraa. To his friend and biographer Robert Graves, Lawrence confessed that he still had a craving to be whipped, that he had been buggered, and that he had enjoyed it. To George Bernard Shaw, Lawrence said that the story in *Seven Pillars* was false, though he did not offer a real version.

The details of the story are certainly full of inconsistencies. In *Seven Pillars,* Lawrence says that he had returned to Aqaba by November 26, which means that, badly injured, he somehow made the trip from Deraa

British commanders present medals after the capture of Jerusalem. Lawrence was present at the ceremony in which the British formally took possession of the holy city, which was for him, he wrote, "the supreme moment of the war."

to Azraq, and from there back to Aqaba, in half the time it usually took. It seems extremely unlikely that the bey, having captured a British officer with a price on his head, would then put him in an unlocked room, with clothes conveniently placed for his escape. And the vividness of the story's details—Lawrence's ability to swivel his head around to see his own back laced with welts, for example, or his careful description of the whip that was brought into the room while he was held down—suggests a greater commitment to imagination than to straightforward description.

The importance of the Deraa story, though, rests not on the details of when or whether it happened, but on the way Lawrence wrote it. Even if real, the story is told like a fantasy. Lawrence is at the center of the action, but he is also at the side of the reader, watching through our eyes. Though face down on the bench, he "sees" the Turks etch lash marks "like the railway"—the symbol of the modern world—into his back. These whiplashes, and the indescribable warmth of sexual arousal they provoke, rupture not only Lawrence's body, but his ability to imagine himself as one with the Arabs. This sexual experience was not the "cold, clean" union of Bedouin in the desert but a town taste, dirty and complicated. For Lawrence to share it is to acknowledge what he shares with the enemy rather than the Arabs, a recognition which in turn makes him more conventionally British. Most other British officers had concluded long before that they shared more with the Turks they were fighting against than with the Arab tribesmen who were supposedly their allies.

The story of Deraa also tempts the reader to consider Lawrence's naked body and the question of what other identity beside his British one lies under his Arab disguise. "You must understand that I know about you," says the bey to the naked young officer, a phrase that in Lawrence's story remains full of unspecified meaning. There is a moment of mutual recognition between Lawrence and the bey: the other men in the room fall back, not party to it. Yet after the rape, Lawrence finds the room he is thrown into unlocked, and upon emerging soon learns that word is not out about his being a British officer. What other secret, then, did the Turkish bey know all about? Could it be the secret of Lawrence's sexual arousal? "Pain of the slightest had been my obsession and secret terror since a boy," Lawrence wrote. "Had I now been drugged with it, to bewilderment?"

Lawrence's other secret—his need to reinvent himself and hide behind the new identity—had also been exposed, at least to Lawrence himself. His trip north had resulted in a bridge being destroyed after all: the one that allowed Lawrence to move comfortably between his British and Arab identities. In the Oxford version of *Seven Pillars,* Lawrence, dragging his wounded body back to Azraq, admits that he feels "maimed, imperfect, only half myself." Nor did he stay long at the castle, choosing instead to hurry back to the English at Aqaba. Was Lawrence's English self too restless to stay on with handsome Ali? Was it with shame, or longing, or both, that he watched the Arab warrior strip off his black robes and ask for Lawrence's white robes in exchange? The two men, *Seven Pillars* records, traded both clothes and a farewell kiss as Lawrence left, embracing like the biblical characters Jonathan and David. Ali, along with Farraj, Daud, and some others, would stay at Azraq, holding the fort, until spring.

Lawrence would go on to acclaim as a soldier, a diplomat, and a writer. A month after Deraa he would stand, in a borrowed British uniform, beside Allenby as the British entered triumphantly into Jerusalem. But from the time of his trip northward, Lawrence's relationship to the Arab revolt would change. He would command only one more solo effort with the Arabs—the triumph of Tafileh, in which he and Feisal's brother Zeid would, in conventional battle, outflank the Turks and take 250 prisoners. Thereafter he would act as one of many British officers in the war effort, commanding British as well as Arab forces. And he would always remember the feeling of Deraa, as described in the Oxford version of *Seven Pillars:* "fascination and terror and morbid desire, lascivious and vicious, perhaps, but like the striving of a moth towards its flame."

Years after the war, in fact, as an enlisted man, Lawrence would explore that fascination further by hiring a fellow soldier, John Bruce, to beat him. Sometimes the beatings were with a birch rod, sometimes with a rope; sometimes they brought Lawrence to the point of orgasm. At other times, Lawrence would have Bruce force him to undergo the deprivations that he had put himself through in his youth—exercising for hours, or swimming in an icy ocean, or going horseback riding until he could hardly move.

Many biographers have found in the story of this relationship, which Bruce sold years later to the London *Times,* something horrible and harmful—not because it was horrible or harmful to Lawrence, but because it went against their sense of what was "good" or "normal." Rarely, however, have those writers distinguished between the kind of pleasure through pain that Lawrence got from Bruce and that which made him a hero: his ability to go without food or sleep for days, to endure great thirst, or ride until his camel dropped.

Was Lawrence's derivation of sexual pleasure from pain an indispensable component of his heroism? That question, ignored by most of Lawrence's moralizing critics, burns like the desert sun at the heart of the Lawrence legend. Lawrence, who never wrote explicitly about his affair with Bruce, is little help on this matter. Perhaps the incident at Deraa was only one of many such experiences, or perhaps a first beating that helped Lawrence realize a lifelong urge. Perhaps the whole thing was made up, an imaginary version of the life Lawrence was living in England as he wrote *Seven Pillars.*

The East, of course, is silent. The bey's family and friends have claimed that the governor was heterosexual and doubt that he—a clever man and a patriot—would have let someone as important as Lawrence escape. But heterosexuals are often involved in male-male rape, and the bey's relatives might not decide to tell the truth. What did the bey himself say about his meeting with Lawrence, if it ever even happened? We will never know. Why? Because in the finest tradition of westerners in the East, nobody ever asked him.

CHAPTER NINE

DAMASCUS OR BUST

I'm in an extraordinary position just now, vis a vis the Sherifs and the tribes and must sooner or later go bust. . . . It is impossible for a foreigner to run another people of their own free will, indefinitely.

—Letter from Lawrence to Clayton, February 1918

As if literalizing the chill that had fallen over Lawrence's fantasy of himself as one with the Arabs, winter came. At outposts stretching north from the Hejaz, the Bedouin struggled to stay warm and hold their captured territory. In the mountains of what is now Jordan, where Lawrence was harrying the Turks with Feisal's brother Zeid, the camels had to walk through blizzards, snowdrifts, and sheets of freezing rain. Often the animals lay down and gave up, not even rising when the men lit fires under them. Lawrence and four companions nearly died themselves as they tried to ride down to Guweira, near Aqaba, to get more gold. The men had to use their bare feet and hands to dig paths through the snow, and blood poured from their frozen, unfeeling flesh. On the way back, Lawrence fell through the ice and landed waist-deep

"With quaint justice, events forced me to live up to my bodyguard, to become as hard, as sudden, as heedless. The odds against me were heavy, and the climate cogged the die." So wrote Lawrence about the situation that faced him following Deraa.

in a swamp of icy mud, surviving only by clutching at the halter of his favorite camel, Woheida, who backed up in terror and pulled him out.

For Lawrence to free himself from the mire of his own doubt proved more difficult. His nerves were shot, he wrote in *Seven Pillars*—he had to "force himself under fire," and he could no longer stand the "posturing in alien dress" and the "preaching in alien speech" to men who trusted him. He even went as far as riding down to Palestine to offer Allenby his resignation, but Hogarth and Clayton, masters of persuasion, were waiting there to reconvince him. He had been awarded a medal for his bravery, they explained. Planes had been out dropping messages for weeks asking him to come in for a consultation. The Allies were preparing another major drive to the north, and it was crucial that Lawrence and Feisal, with both Bedouin and British camel soldiers behind them, be ready to protect the English army's lengthening eastern flank.

The British were willing to pay gold to keep the Arabs turned against the Turks—this was war, and they had no time to worry if the strategy would also cost Lawrence his peace of mind. So, like a mythical king or a tragic stage heroine, Lawrence drew his silk robes over his anxieties and made ready for his audiences. At Guweira, Lawrence offered Feisal words of encouragement and the promise of British reinforcements. In Jerusalem, he chatted with his old friend Ronald Storrs, now military governor of the city, and with the American journalist Lowell Thomas, who was the governor's guest. In Cairo, Lawrence greeted Hubert Young, the understudy chosen to replace him if he were captured or killed, with the breezy advice that the job was "amusing" and offered "plenty of honor and glory to be picked up without any great difficulty." "There was no escape for me," Lawrence wrote in *Seven Pillars*. "I must take up again my mantle of fraud in the East. . . . It might be fraud or it might be farce: no one should say that I could not play it."

Lawrence, however, would no longer play his part quietly, or alone. Whenever possible he traveled with an entourage he called his bodyguard, 90 of the hardest, toughest Arab adolescents he could find. Again, Lawrence's descriptions of his bodyguard seemed strikingly revealing of himself: he called them young men "full of carnal passion" but also able to "find pleasure in subordination." The men drew standard army salary, but Lawrence mounted them on his personal camels, the finest in Aqaba. In return he demanded absolute obedience and the ability to make ready for a six-week trip in half an hour, to ride without any baggage camels, and to travel day and night. Nearly 60 of these young men would die in his service.

Lawrence's outfits were nothing compared to his bodyguards'. Much to his delight, they dressed in outrageous waistcoats of polka dots and green and orange stripes. "My bodyguard . . . picked riders of the young men of the desert, are more splendid than a tulip garden," he wrote to Vivyan Richards. The leader of the group, Abdullah El-Nahabi

Lawrence's raiders cross the desert. "I had to have with me picked riders, on my own beasts," he wrote. "We bought at long prices the fastest and strongest camels to be obtained. We chose them for speed and power, no matter how hard and exhausting they might be under the saddle."

(Abdullah the Robber), had three braids, a "sensual, loose, wet" mouth and a reputation for having been whipped and jailed by every Arabian prince in the desert. He kept discipline among the bodyguards with savage force, but he trained the camels to come by name and take gifts of bread from his moist lips. Many mounts came running from a hundred yards when the members of Lawrence's bodyguard called their names. The other Arabs at Aqaba would have been tempted to run away. "The men called them cutthroats, but they cut throats only to my order," Lawrence observed with satisfaction.

Once again, Lawrence was using the Arabs as a shield to ward off easy analysis by his British colleagues. "Yallah, Imshee. Ma feesh bakhsheesh!" (Beat it! We have no spare change!) English soldiers at Aqaba would jeer with characteristic condescension as the Bedouin approached, and then fall into stunned silence as the leader pulled down his head cloth to reveal the calm, cold eyes of Colonel Lawrence. Lawrence, on the other hand, as biographers Malcolm Brown and Julia Cave have written, treated even lower-ranking British soldiers with unusual respect. He would address new arrivals company by company, explaining that he relied on their "Western understanding" to help them avoid conflicts with the Bedouin. Major W. F. Stirling listened to Lawrence give the men "the straightest talk I have ever heard" about self-restraint, and explain that in return he was going to take them through a part of Arabia where no man had set foot since the time of the Crusades. The men were delighted, recalled Stirling, and "retired for the night . . . fully convinced that they were about to embark on the greatest jaunt in the history of war."

But what did Lawrence feel as he led a wave of clumsy English camel riders into the valleys of Rumm? The desert where he had once delighted in being out of reach of British schoolboys in shorts was now full of them. Their camels, he wrote in *Seven Pillars,* rattled with twenty accoutrements, in contrast to the single saddlebag the Bedouin threw on in one easy motion. He found the brows of the British low and their gaze weak beside "the fine-drawn Arabs whom generations of inbreeding had sharpened to a radiance ages older than the primitive, blotched, honest Englishmen." And yet Lawrence knew that he was one of the latter. His Orientalist dream—of the westerner alone with the natives—was evaporating.

Lawrence's sense of the clean, gallant sexuality of the revolt, and the young men who best embodied it, was also fading. Riding northward on reconnaissance, he was met by his trusted servant Farraj, whose usually smiling face was dark and hard. Daud was dead, frozen to death at Azraq, he told Lawrence. Farraj would stay with Lawrence, taking greater care than ever as he tended to his camels, coffee, and saddles, but his laughter would never return. Even after other men offered themselves to him, according to *Seven Pillars,* Farraj stayed alone and withdrawn.

Less than a month later, while riding near an enemy patrol, Farraj suddenly turned and drove his camel toward the Turks. Lawrence and the bodyguard cried out in warning, but Farraj galloped on. They found him lying in the grass half-conscious, his spine smashed by a bullet, with a company of Turks heading straight toward him. Moving Farraj was clearly impossible, so Lawrence knelt beside him, holding his pistol flat so that the boy would not guess what he was about to do. Farraj opened his eyes and flashed his old, merry look. "Daud will be angry with you," he whispered, smiling, as he took Lawrence's hand. "Salute him for me," Lawrence replied sadly, and pulled the trigger. Later that day, when the bodyguards started to fight over Farraj's camel, Lawrence killed her, too.

Lawrence did whatever was necessary to keep peace in the ranks—pressing Allenby for more camels; keeping British soldiers and tribesmen from squabbling; reiterating Allied promises of Arab independence. When Feisal opened secret talks with the Turks, Lawrence bribed the Arab leader's aides to keep him apprised of the situation. When Hussein accused Feisal of falling under British sway, Lawrence made sure he got the telegrams first: he doctored some, suppressed others, and patched together an agreement between father and son.

But when it came to reconciling his own warring feelings, Lawrence showed none of the same skills. According to *Seven Pillars,* he spent August 15, 1918—his thirtieth birthday—lost in doubt. "Here were

Lawrence (on foot) with some of the members of his personal bodyguard. "I needed hard riders and hard livers; men proud of themselves and without family," he wrote in describing the criteria for membership in this elite corps.

Arabs believing in me, Allenby trusting me, my bodyguard dying for me: and I began to wonder if all established reputations were founded, like myself, on fraud," he wrote.

Was Lawrence's pain that of the secret agent, or the homosexual? His book does not really say, but 75 years later, many gay men and lesbians use practically the same words to talk about what sounds like the same sense of hypocrisy. Their dilemma, though, is "coming out"—deciding to reveal their true sexuality in public. "From the beginning I had avoided dealing with my sexuality, but . . . now it felt like a lie—a lie whose perpetuation was beginning to sicken me, to eat away at my soul," Joseph Steffan, a 19-year-old student at Annapolis Naval Academy, wrote in 1992, describing his recognition of the fact that he loved and wanted to be loved by men. Many others, of all ages, have described a similar crisis of confidence that preceded their decision to acknowledge that they were gay or lesbian.

Lawrence tried to wash away his pain in battle. On September 19, 1918, Allenby's cannons opened up holes too big to ever be closed in the Turkish lines in Palestine. British infantry poured through, and cavalry, racing north, cut east toward Damascus shortly after. By the second day of fighting, the Allies had the Turks in the middle of a giant claw of troops that was slowly closing round Syria. The only route of escape lay to the east, where Lawrence and Feisal, with help from Bedouin warriors, British planes, and trained troops, were already closing the last escape routes. Lawrence leapt from planes to cars to camels, coordinating Feisal's forces and news of other Allied movements. Dozens of pounds fell from his already trim body under the strain. But on September 23 the town of Maan, where Turkish defenders had held off the Bedouin for a year, surrendered. By the 27th, the Turks in Deraa, site of Lawrence's humiliation, were in retreat. The tribesmen swarmed in after them, killing every Turk they could find.

Even Lawrence was drawn into the bloodlust. A British plane dropped word of a Turkish column retreating through the village of Tafas, north of Deraa. When Lawrence and the others arrived, they looked in horror at the savagery: a pregnant woman speared to the ground by bayonets; a little girl lanced in the neck. When they found the Turks, Auda and Lawrence led the charge, with the Englishman giving the order to take no prisoners. "In the madness born of the horror of Tafas we killed and killed, even blowing in the heads of the fallen and the animals; as though their death and running blood could slake our agony," he wrote.

But death would fuel, not quench, Lawrence's agony. Even as Arab victory seemed near, he learned that his beloved Salim Ahmed—Dahoum—had fallen seriously ill. Tom Beaumont, a British gunner who served under Lawrence and was interviewed by his biographers Phillip Knightley and Colin Simpson, recalled his commander's devastation when he returned from a trip with the bodyguard. "I said to him 'Did you see Salim?' and he said, 'It's finished. He's dying.'. . . Lawrence turned away and pulled his kuffiye [head cloth] over his face and I heard him say, 'I loved that boy.' When he turned back I could see that he had been weeping. I overheard the bodyguards talking and I caught the Arabic word for death and I saw them make gestures like Lawrence holding Salim in his arms."

Deprived of the man who had inspired his role in the Arab revolt, Lawrence turned his passion toward the object of the revolt itself: Damascus. The British had said that the Arabs could lay claim to all territories that they liberated without Allied help, and Lawrence was determined to see Feisal's forces take the city. One of his English colleagues, Alec Kirkbride, remembered Lawrence staring straight ahead in those days, eyes unseeing, as he pushed forward in the armored Rolls Royce he called the Blue Mist. Hoisting Hussein's flag in towns along the road to Damascus, Lawrence kept muttering: "We must get there before the cavalry!"

The Blue Mist would roar into Damascus, and controversy, on October 1. Hussein's flag was already flying there, hoisted by the city residents themselves. The Australian cavalry was there too, as were many of Feisal's Bedouin. Who got there first, and who should serve as governor, would become hotly debated issues, but according to *Seven*

Lawrence enters Damascus in the Blue Mist on October 1, 1918. "My memory of the entry into Damascus," he wrote to fellow officer W. F. Stirling in 1924, "was of a quietness and emptiness of street, and of myself crying like a baby with eventual thankfulness, in the Blue Mist by your side."

Pillars there was no doubt whom Damascus residents wanted in charge. Hundreds of thousands of people jammed the streets to welcome Feisal's forces, showering Lawrence and Feisal's other allies with rosewater, flowers, and cheers. From every side, Lawrence wrote in *Seven Pillars,* the women of Damascus trilled the traditional "a-la-la-la-la-la" of celebration. The deep, measured chants of the men rolled along the narrow streets and ancient walls of the city, building to a roar of welcome for Feisal and his advisers: Feisal! Nasir! Shukri! Urens!

But the most important arrivals, Lawrence knew, were yet to be made. It was not until October 3 that Allenby's gray Rolls Royce pulled up to the Victoria Hotel in Damascus; several hours later Feisal himself arrived. Lawrence acted as interpreter at that first meeting of the two most important men in the Arabian campaign, but even so, communication was not good. Allenby coldly informed Feisal that neither Lebanon nor Palestine would fall under his control and that he could rule the rest of Syria only with a French liaison at his side. When Feisal objected, Allenby turned to Lawrence. "But did you not tell him that the French were to have the Protectorate over Syria?" "No Sir, I know nothing about it," Lawrence answered. Lawrence was stretching the truth, of course; Feisal had never been *officially* informed of the secret British-French agreement on that point, but Lawrence had told him about it long before.

But the British, with their promises of Arab independence, had lied far more directly. The Turkish ammunition stores in Damascus were still burning, the flash of powder and the taste of smoke was still in the air, and Lawrence's fears of British betrayal of the Arabs were coming true. "I think I had better go back to England," Lawrence said to Allenby after Feisal left, explaining that he would never serve with a French representative. "Yes, I think you better had!" Allenby snapped back. To biographer Lidell Hart, Lawrence breezed over the painful separation with a one-liner: "Never outstay a climax," but he closed *Seven Pillars* with a more sentimental and revealing version: "I made to Allenby the last (and also I think the first) request I ever made him for myself—leave to go away. . . . He agreed; and then at once I knew how much I was sorry."

CHAPTER TEN

WAR AT THE PEACE CONFERENCE

Do make clear . . . that my objects were to save England, and France too, from the follies of the imperialists. . . . I think, though there's a great future for the British Empire as a voluntary association.

—Letter from Lawrence to an academic studying the Arab revolt, 1928

Both Lawrence (on steps, third from right) and Feisal (center) attended the Paris Peace Conference in 1919. Feisal, Lawrence wrote, was "very gentle . . . and very kind, and very considerate, and outrageously generous to his friends, and mild to his enemies, and clean and honest and intelligent: and full of wild freakish humor."

Powder flashed and smoke rose over Paris in January 1919—not from guns this time, but from the old-fashioned cameras recording the arrivals of the dignitaries. President Woodrow Wilson came by boat, the first time in history that an American chief executive had gone abroad while in office. Prime Minister Lloyd George of England and his entourage were there, racing over the Paris boulevards in a fleet of army cars. Princes, generals, young soldiers and old colonial hands—Lawrence and Feisal among them—filled the drawing rooms of the big hotels, gossiping, scheming, arguing, and agreeing. This was the Paris Peace Conference, where for six months the winners of the war wrangled over the punishments to be imposed on the losers, apportioned the war's spoils, and tried to pick up the pieces after the most shattering conflict in western history.

Lawrence moved impatiently through the ceremonies, turning abruptly when the conversation bored him or seemed to hold no promise. Behind the orderly hearings and polite parties—the British delegation alone filled five hotels and dined at tables that glittered with wit and crystal—he could discern a contest of strength more like a street brawl. To the victors belong the spoils, the saying goes, and in the Middle East and elsewhere, victorious France and Britain both intended to extract payment for their efforts. "What do you want in the Middle East?" Prime Minister Georges Clemenceau of France had whispered to Lloyd George at a reception the month before. "I want [the city of] Mosul attached to Iraq, and Palestine under British control," George replied. "You shall have it," Clemenceau was said to have responded, "but we need Syria." Lawrence had to fight to even get Feisal invited to the Paris negotiations, and Lawrence himself was hardly welcome. "Show him he is on the wrong path," the French instructed their Middle East experts. "If he comes here as a British Colonel in British uniform . . . we shall welcome him. But we shall not accept him if he comes as an Arab and remains disguised as such."

Who was going to welcome the Arabs? And what spoils would go to the victors who were not European? Those were the questions that the young, virtually unknown Colonel Lawrence, first in England and now in Paris, was raising at every opportunity. Britain and the Middle East would both benefit, Lawrence insisted, if Feisal were made king of Syria and his brothers Abdullah and Zeid given control of upper and lower Mesopotamia. In London, Lawrence had even testified before the prestigious Eastern Committee—headed by the legendary ex-viceroy of India, Lord Curzon—where he said flat out that the Sykes-Picot Agreement, which promised Syria to France, should be ignored.

For support in his campaign, Lawrence turned to what today might seem an unlikely ally: the Zionists, as those who were working for the establishment of an independent Jewish state were known. When Feisal visited London in December 1918, Lawrence worked with the British Foreign Office to arrange a meeting between him and Chaim Weizmann, the brilliant Jewish chemist who was the leader of England's Zionist movement. Like Feisal, Weizmann had been promised a place in the Middle East by the British government—a "homeland" where the Jews of Europe could immigrate, set up schools, and make new lives for themselves away from discrimination and violence. Unlike Feisal, Weizmann had neither land nor the loyalty of the local Arab inhabitants. With Lawrence acting as interpreter, the Arab prince and the Jewish chemist reached an agreement: Feisal would recognize the right of the Jews to live in Palestine, so long as the immigrants did not take away land inhabited by the Arabs or insist on an all-Jewish government. The Jews, in return, would provide Feisal with moral support at the peace conference, and with significant financial support shortly thereafter. The principles of this agreement, with no mention of the finances, were set to paper on January 3, 1919, and both men signed. Lawrence had brokered the first Arab-Jewish peace accord in Palestine.

Even George V, king of England, found himself the object of Lawrence's campaign to establish Feisal and his brothers as rulers in the Middle East. Invited to Buckingham Palace to receive the medals he had been awarded during the war, Lawrence unceremoniously told his monarch that he could not accept them. It became one of Lawrence's own favorite anecdotes: the king turning to pick up another medal, only to find that Lawrence had torn off the one he had just pinned on. "Colonel Lawrence said that he had pledged his word to Feisal, and that now the British Government were about to let down the Arabs," read the court's account of the meeting. Later, in Paris, Lawrence would amuse himself with other ill-mannered expressions of dissatisfaction: standing on a stairwell, for example, and showering toilet paper on Lloyd George, foreign secretary David Balfour, and Lord Hardinge. "There is nothing funny about toilet paper," Hardinge was heard to remark in consternation, but as the sheets wafted down Lawrence was hidden safely behind the banister, laughing his head off. If the prank was a childish way of criticizing his superiors, it also evoked the worthlessness of the other private papers—the secret treaties, letters of

Delegates to the Cairo Peace Conference of 1921 pose in front of the pyramids. Lawrence (fifth rider from left) was more pleased with the outcome at Cairo than he had been with the decisions made at Paris, for he was able to help secure a throne for Feisal as ruler of the new kingdom of Iraq.

understanding, and wartime promises—that were in danger of being flushed down the toilet as the Allies bargained with each other to create a new world order.

In actuality, the Middle East was a minor detail at the peace conference, where the biggest concern of the Allies was how much money they could squeeze out of defeated Germany for "reparations." And there was plenty of damage to repair: the Ottoman, the German,

the Austro-Hungarian, and the Russian empires had all been pulled down by the time the war ended in November 1918. A staggering 50 million soldiers and civilians had been killed. Even in the Middle Eastern sphere, Lawrence and Feisal were only a few of the many voices clamoring for a settlement, and they were among the least powerful.

So once again Lawrence fell back on his secret weapon—Arab clothing. In the Hejaz, Lawrence could claim that he had worn his costume to blend in, but in Paris he dressed to draw attention. He wore full Arab dress to a party; for meetings, he threw a green silk veil with tassels of deep red over his explorer's helmet and cinched it with a deep red cord. Accompanied by Feisal, who wore full Arab dress and whose room was guarded by two huge Nubians with swords, Lawrence's garb certainly grabbed attention from others in attendance. "That younger successor of Muhammad, Colonel Lawrence," commented James Shotwell, a young American from Columbia University, was "the most winning figure, so every one says, at the whole peace conference."

Shotwell's praises, echoed by Lowell Thomas later that year, caught the special appeal Lawrence always held for Americans. Like Lawrence, the Americans were new to the European power game, full of dreams and aspirations and unconstrained by the old rules of proper behavior and aristocratic exchange. President Wilson, with whom Lawrence and Feisal had lunch, had already set Europe talking with his "Fourteen Points" of diplomacy, which included a ban on secret agreements and the right of all peoples to self-determination. But while Wilson and Shotwell were being bowled over by Lawrence, the Oxford-educated, ever-so-respectable Lord Curzon was puzzling over the phrase "fed up," which he had read in one of Lawrence's official cables. "What's fed up?" the last of the great imperial secretaries is said to have asked in annoyance. "I believe, my Lord, that it is equivalent of disgruntled," responded an aide. "Ah," said Curzon, "I suppose it is a term in use among the middle classes."

But Lawrence's classiness was indisputable on February 6, when Prince Feisal ibn El Hussein and his "interpreter" Colonel Lawrence—dressed, as Lloyd George remembered, in "flowing robes of dazzling white"—received a hearing before the Council of Ten. Comprised of five presidents or prime ministers and their foreign secretaries, the Council of Ten was the most powerful body at the conference, and Lawrence and Feisal had prepared their speeches carefully. Suspicious of Lawrence's translation, the French had their own interpreter present, but even they were struck by the eloquence and bearing of the delicate Arab prince and the young English soldier. Suddenly, though, as distinguished historian Arnold Toynbee remembered it, there was a hitch—the Italians had understood neither the Arabic nor the English:

> President Wilson then made a suggestion. "Colonel Lawrence," he said, "could you put the Amir Feisal's statement into French now for us?" After a moment Lawrence started off and did it; and when he came to the end of this unprepared piece of translation the Ten clapped. What had happened was amazing. Lawrence's spell had made the Ten forget, for a moment, who they were and what they were supposed to be doing. They had started the session as conscious arbiters of the destinies of mankind; they were ending it as captive audience of a minor suppliant's interpreter.

It was one of the last spells that Lawrence would cast for his prince, and it would soon be broken. Both Lawrence and Feisal would be forced to leave the conference early: Lawrence to attend to his father, who was dying of influenza, and Feisal to prepare for a visit from an American commission whose recommendations would be totally ignored. The French and British, left to their own negotiations, would each get what they had agreed upon in that cocktail reception before the conference: a "mandate" for the British in Mesopotamia, and one for the French in Syria. For the British, that meant a right to the increasingly important oil fields of what is today Iraq. For the French, it meant the right to kick Feisal out of Damascus, which they did in July 1920. For Lawrence, it meant hypocrisy and failure. "The old men came out again and took our victory," he wrote in the preface to *Seven Pillars*. "Youth could win, but had not learned to keep."

The "lost generation" was what the British called the thousands of young men cut down in World War I, but the term could also describe the young men who survived. Lawrence was one of many for whom the war was followed by an overwhelming feeling that some sense of order had been "taken away," lost forever. That sense of alienation lay just under the surface of the art the surrealists were making in Paris, was audible in the drifting monologues of English writers like Virginia Woolf, and burst through the prose of *Seven Pillars* as regularly as did sharp rocks and battle cries. Loss was also central to the legend of how *Seven Pillars* was written: no sooner had Lawrence completed a first draft of the manuscript than the entire thing, including all photographs and notes, was stolen from him in a London railway station. Loss was carved into the stones of the Oxford buildings where Lawrence went to rewrite the book, etched into the memorial tablets and brass plaques put up at every college to commemorate the fallen of World War I. "In a time when the undergraduate population was never more than 3,000," wrote British historian Jan Morris, "nearly 2,700 members of the University had been killed in that war."

Dead, too, was a sense of obligation to the group ideal, the collective life of the empire. "Sons be welded each and all,/ Into one imperial whole,/ One with Britain, heart and soul!" Alfred Lord Tennyson had written in a poem popular during Lawrence's childhood, but neither being a son nor a part of the empire seemed to mean as much 20 years later. Lawrence returned to Oxford after the peace conference, but not to his family's house—he chose instead to accept rooms at All Souls College, where he had been offered a prestigious fellowship, complete with stipend, to write a book. The university did not satisfy him, however, and he spent most of his time writing in a rented attic room in London, where he could be anonymous. He still enjoyed schoolboy pranks—he ran the Hejaz flag up the flagpole at All Souls, and hung a bell captured from a Turkish railway station out his window—but such gestures of victory and high spirits rang a little hollow in the postwar atmosphere, where the grand assumptions of the empire had been clouded by doubt. "How long will we permit millions of pounds, thousands of imperial troops and tens of thousands of Arabs to be sacrificed on behalf of a colonial form of administration that can benefit nobody but its administrators?" Lawrence wondered in the Sunday *Times* after the Iraqis rose up in rebellion against their British masters.

A lack of faith in civilization, constant self-questioning, and a heightened sense of the individual psyche are a few of the features that critics refer to when they talk about "modernity." And many would come to see Lawrence as a modern hero, not so much for his wartime exploits as because he withdrew to the realm of art and the self to explore their meaning. In the year after the peace conference he wrote for 15 or even 20 hours a day, not pausing even to eat, staying up all night, and throwing on coveralls to keep himself warm in his unheated attic room. His lack of attention to personal comforts was more than made up for, however, in the obsessive attention he paid to the details of writing and publication. He decided to print the book in the old style that he and Vivyan Richards had dreamed of in college: each chapter had to begin with an illuminated letter, and each page had to end in a complete sentence at the bottom right-hand corner. There could be no blank space at the end of any chapter. These demands would mean hours of rewriting, and Lawrence would look at some printer's proofs more than a dozen times before he deemed

Lawrence (center, in homburg) and other delegates to the Cairo Peace Conference, in Amman, the capital city of the newly created British mandate of Transjordan, where Abdullah (front row, right, in dark robes), Feisal's brother, ruled as emir.

a page finished. It was as if by controlling the words, he hoped to rewrite reality.

Art was the one area where Lawrence still dared to dream. He revived both his friendship with Richards and their plan to begin a Morris-style printing press, and the two bought some land together in Epping Forest. The "book-to-build-the-house" Lawrence called *Seven Pillars,* and his room at All Souls was soon full of drawings he commissioned for his own volume. He avoided the admirers created by the Lowell Thomas show but was happy to sit for paintings and sculptures or to use his reputation to meet great artists. It was during this second Oxford period that T. E. met the famous novelist Thomas Hardy, as well as the young World War I veteran and poet Robert Graves. Hardy would become a lifelong friend, and Graves both a friend and biographer. "I've always stood in the plain, like an ant hill, watching the mountain and wanting to be one," Lawrence wrote to E. M. Forster, another famous writer and friend he made just after this time at Oxford, explaining his decision to put down his pistol and take up the pen.

Forster, a shy, not-so-handsome Cambridge man who had worked in Egypt during the war, was in a good position to understand the material Lawrence was trying to fashion into a book. Forster had also experienced interracial, homosexual love—first as a tutor to a stunningly handsome Indian named Syed Ross Masood in England and later while serving as secretary to the maharaja of the Indian state of Dewas. *Seven Pillars,* in fact, was one of the books Forster would read before finishing his own book about love and pain at the end of the colonial era, the acclaimed *Passage to India.* Forster's book, like *Seven Pillars,* contains a famous rape scene, this time with a woman victim, in which the reader cannot tell if the rape is imagined or real. As in *Seven Pillars,* the rape in *Passage to India* becomes an expression of the break between the English and the native population, a figure for the inevitable souring of the colonial harmony. Unlike Lawrence's book, in which the desert unites the author and the men he loves, the physical surroundings in Forster's novel are a reminder of the impossibility of intimacy between a British man and a man from the colonies. "Why can't we be friends now?," the E. M. Forster–like character Fielding says to his Indian friend Aziz in the last paragraph of *Passage to India,* holding him affectionately:

> "It's what I want. It's what you want."
>
> But the horses didn't want it—they swerved apart; the earth didn't want it, sending up rocks through which riders must pass single file; the temples, the tank, the jail, the palace, the birds, the carrion, the guest house, that came into view as they issued from the gap . . . they didn't want it, they said in their hundred voices, "No, not yet," and the sky said, "No, not there."

And when and where would Lawrence hold his own beloved, or share the secrets of his own sexual longings? The chances in the new, modern England were many: Forster and Richards were only two of the men Lawrence knew who might have been willing to share their own confidences, or perhaps their bodies, with him. John Maynard Keynes, the brilliant young economist who had sat opposite Lawrence at the Eastern Committee, was homosexual. The good-looking and muscular David Garnett, who was to be the editor of Lawrence's letters, slept with men—he had enjoyed a long affair with the soon-to-be famous painter Duncan Grant. Forster, Keynes, Garnett, and Grant were all part of the Bloomsbury group, a social set named after the London neighborhood they lived in, where many writers and artists lived in openly homosexual relationships of various durations. Virginia Woolf, her once-girlfriend Vita Sackville-West, the writer Lytton Strachey, who had slept with Keynes and Grant—they were all living and discussing the new sexual freedoms only a few minutes away from where Lawrence was starving himself in his cold attic. Many of them belonged to what they called the "Memoir Club," which would meet three or four times a year at a different member's home to read autobiographical papers that had to be of absolute frankness. Lawrence's confessions, including his discussion of the rape, would certainly have been met there more with curiosity than with condemnation.

But Lawrence did not feel himself made for the Memoir Club, or for confession. His politics, for one thing, were not the leftist ones of Bloomsbury—though disillusioned with the government, he still had hopes that a throne might yet be found for Feisal. Lawrence might sketch out his sexual preferences on paper, but in person he was like his parents: preferring to conceal rather than reveal. "I wanted to read your long novel, but was afraid to," he wrote to Forster years later, after refusing to read Forster's explicitly homosexual book *Maurice*. "If I read it, I had you, and supposing I hadn't liked it? I'm so funnily made up, sexually. At present you are in all respects right, in my eyes: that's because you reserve so very much, as I do. If you knew all about me (perhaps you do: your subtlety is very great: shall I put it 'if I knew that you knew?') . . . you'd think very little of me."

Lawrence did read a short story of Forster's about homosexual love and found in it exactly what he had seen in the love affair between Farraj and Daud and never seemed able to find in himself: purity. "There is a strange cleansing beauty about the whole piece of writing. So passionate of course: so indecent, people might say: but I must confess that it has made me change my point of view. I suppose you will not print it? . . . The Turks, as you probably know . . . did it to me, by force: and since then I have gone about whimpering to myself 'unclean, unclean.' Now I don't know. Perhaps there is another side, your side, to the story."

Politically, Lawrence would find a way to cleanse himself, agreeing in 1921 to join Winston Churchill's Colonial Office and working to forge a new settlement in the Middle East. For months, Lawrence met with other English experts and hammered out a plan that was signed, with some fanfare, at a 1921 conference in Cairo. "Practically all the experts and authorities on the Middle East were summoned," Churchill wrote of the conference, though as historian Jan Morris points out, 36 of the 38 participants were British. Hussein, outraged at this latest intervention, would refuse to accept it and would be deposed as king of the Hejaz in 1924. Feisal, on the other hand, would get a throne after all, as the king of troubled Iraq, where he would reign until 1933 with a series of English advisers at his side. His brother, Abdullah, with Lawrence's fellow soldier Alec Kirkbride as his advisor, would be given what is now the kingdom of Jordan, where his grandson, King Hussein, still holds power today. Lawrence, who chose not to play the role of adviser to either court, seemed relieved to be done with the whole business. "I must put on record my conviction," he wrote, "that England is out of the Arab affair with clean hands."

His sexual conscience, however, would be less easily cleared. Many who had found romance in the East, like Forster, turned to working-class Englishmen to fill the void left by the Arabs and Indians they had loved in the past. Forster's lovers in England, for example, were bus drivers and policemen, security guards and window cleaners. The playwright and former junior officer Joe Ackerly, a close friend of Forster's, had slept with young Indian men while serving as secretary to the maharaja of Chatarpur, but in England he shared his bed with a rough, attractive sailor. Air Commodore Leo Charlton, former chief of air staff in Iraq, had an ex-aircraftman for a lover. These men socialized together, talked about their exploits, and used their boyfriends to find their friends boyfriends.

Yet Lawrence did not feel free to do the same. By 1923, he had scrapped his plans to open the press with Vivyan Richards. Since Dahoum, he later acknowledged, he had found no one to whom he felt able to open himself completely. And he certainly did not seem to want to talk about his sexuality with other homosexuals. "The impulse strong enough to make me touch another creature has not yet been born in me," he wrote to Forster in 1927.

What Lawrence did not tell Forster is that by that time he had found young John Bruce to act as both his disciplinarian and his sexual partner: in other words, that Lawrence needed the "impulses" for sex to come from without rather than from within. Like Forster and Ackerly, Lawrence would venture to a working-class setting to confront his homosexuality; unlike them, he would not remove himself at the end of the evening. Rather, he would submerge himself, shocking and surprising his many fashionable friends. Though he told Hogarth that he was gathering material for a book, there was something much deeper at work when Lawrence gave up his job, changed his name to Ross, and used his connections to enlist anonymously as a private in the air force. The officer and the gentleman was about to become an unknown soldier.

RK4907

CHAPTER ELEVEN

IN THE ARMY NOW

I vant to be alone.

—film star Greta Garbo

The poor soul. I feel for her.

—T. E. Lawrence, about Greta Garbo

The Mint, Lawrence's book about his experience in the Royal Air Force, opens with four simple words: "God, this is awful." One paragraph later, would-be-recruit Lawrence, name newly changed to Ross, is standing naked and obedient before his medical examiners. "'Now jump. . . . lift your right leg. . . . cough. . . . on your toes. . . turn round: bend over. Hullo, what the hell's those marks? Punishment?'" "No, Sir," Lawrence replies, "more like persuasion, Sir, I think."

Lawrence atop the fifth Boanerges, as he named his Brough Superior motorcyles. There would be eight in all; frequent accidents and hard use made it necessary for him to often replace them. "A skittish motor-bike with a touch of blood in it is better than all the riding animals in the world," he wrote in *The Mint.*

Punishment, or persuasion? That question, written into Lawrence's back by the whiplashes he received at Deraa, runs also through every page of *The Mint,* and through every day that Lawrence spent as a soldier in Britain's military. For nearly 10 years Lawrence lay in huts, polished buttons, cleaned kitchens, fixed machines, and took orders. When the scandal of a national hero serving as a lowly air force recruit was discovered—"Uncrowned King as Private Soldier!" crowed the *Daily Express* newspaper—Lawrence was expelled, but not defeated. He changed his name again, to Shaw, appealed to friends in the War Office, and reenlisted in the Royal Tank Corps. Several years later he got himself back into the air force. His colleagues were young and rough, and on more than one occasion beat and bloodied him. John Bruce, at Lawrence's own request, disciplined him with a birch rod across the buttocks. But was it a punishment Lawrence felt he deserved, or a tactic he created to persuade himself to do what he really wanted to do? Was Lawrence atoning, or enjoying? Was there a difference?

The Mint takes its name from the place where governments melt down metal and make new, shining coins. And there can be no doubt that Lawrence liked the idea of liquidating his own high-profile role and being recast as a smaller, cleaner part of the power of the British realm. But unlike a coin or a 20-year-old recruit, Lawrence had a complicated history, and meltdown could not be achieved so cleanly. His guilty conscience, and his glamour, would stay with him no matter where he was stationed. "I want to dirty myself outwardly, so that my person may properly reflect the dirtiness which it conceals," Lawrence wrote in a letter to Charlotte Shaw, wife of the famous playwright George Bernard Shaw, though his confession was contradicted by its context. Because no matter how much he claimed he wanted to blacken himself out of history, Lawrence was still writing letters and paying visits, making sure that he had a place in the address books and dining rooms of the powerful. He would sit in the barracks rooms, blanket drawn up around his knees, dashing off correspondence to a list of recipients that included George Bernard Shaw, Thomas Hardy, head of the air force Hugh Trenchard, and member of Parliament and fantastically wealthy socialite Lady Astor.

In polite society, Lawrence's decision to withdraw from the limelight only accentuated the eccentric allure that had always been part of his social life. "The mystery man of Europe and Asia," the tabloids would call Lawrence, who would often drop in unexpectedly on famous friends and then vanish just as suddenly. His uniform was a cover for quite irregular, even rude, behavior. One moment Lawrence would be chatting knowledgeably about art and literature, and the next sitting silently at the table and refusing the five courses the hosts had prepared, claiming that he was on military rations. Nor, as biographer Lawrence James noted, did Lawrence ever lose his pleasure in behavior that caught the neighbors up short. "Very democratic, aren't we," a French visitor observed snootily to Thomas Hardy, seeing a khaki-wearing Lawrence at his side. "I'm sorry, Mr. Hardy doesn't understand French," Lawrence snapped back in French. "May I offer myself as an interpreter?"

But Lawrence's decision to enlist was also a way of getting back to "foreign" service, a ticket out of the dinner party circuit and into less familiar territory. "The notion of a crusade, of a body of men leaving one country to do noble deeds in another . . . never left him . . . at one time it was Arabia, later on it was the Air," E. M. Forster wrote of Lawrence, in a line that captured the romance of the air force in the eyes of the English. Few people had ever flown in airplanes in those days, and being connected with them had something of the glamour of being an astronaut today. But for Lawrence, that romance was matched by the equally attractive idea of finding a place in a setting that people like the Hardys and the Shaws could never hope to feel comfortable. The barracks, like the desert, were a world of their own.

"Our hut is a fair microcosm of unemployed England," Lawrence wrote in *The Mint,* and he went on to describe characters as exotic in their own way as Auda or Feisal. One of these was Sailor, a powerful, deep-voiced man who moved "like quicksilver" on his feet and was a "master" with his fists and his curses. Sailor was the leader of the "hut"—the corrugated iron shack in which Lawrence and 49 other recruits slept, only an arm's length apart, on rock-hard beds set on a bare cement floor. His constant companion was China, a stocky, snarling fighter. The sneers and swearing that came out of both men's mouths and their constant comments about sex riveted Lawrence, who had never been so close to such coarseness. Sailor and China, he wrote, "fascinate me with the attraction of unlikeness: for I think I fear animal spirits more than anything in the world."

Animal spirit—male animal spirit—pervades *The Mint* and Lawrence's accounts of life in the military. Men lying on beds, telling dirty jokes, pulling at each other's clothes in the stifling heat, wrestling and cursing and crowding together in bathrooms with no doors—this was the new landscape in which Lawrence tried to find his way. At night the men got drunk, sang lewd songs, and joked loudly about sex and "blanket drill"—their word for masturbation—leaving the prudish Lawrence with no place to escape his shame. Gone, too, were the adoring nicknames like Prince Dynamite and al-Aurans: "Shortarse" was what the men of the barracks called Lawrence. Even their lower-class accents were like foreign dialects, and Lawrence—much to the annoyance of some of his Oxford colleagues—practiced speaking in "garage English" in much the same way he had practiced his Arabic years before.

Just as in the desert, Lawrence never really passed as one of the others: within months, most of the recruits knew his real identity. And just as in the desert, Lawrence focused on clothes as a way of simultaneously covering up and calling attention to the political and erotic complexities of the situation. "Boys in fancy dress, for the first time, went stroking and smoothing their thighs," Lawrence wrote, describing the day the recruits received the blue uniforms of the Royal Air Men. "The tailors had taken [the trousers] in at the knees, by our secret request, so tightly that they gripped the flesh and had a riding cut." But while battle uniform seemed safe when Lawrence was far away in the Middle East, in England such dandyish dress seemed to Lawrence to be an uncomfortable reminder of the homosexuality that was so often its companion: "These clothes are too tight. At every pace they catch us in a dozen joints of the body, and remind us of it. . . . They provoke lasciviousness, by telling so much of ourselves."

For Lawrence, the telling of oneself was better left for writing. At night, exhausted from long days of cleaning, drilling, and doing exercises, he scribbled down notes for *The Mint* and revisions for the yet-to-be-published *Seven Pillars,* writing on single sheets of paper and telling the other soldiers that he was writing letters. Each book's tone was radically different—*Seven Pillars* has a prose style as flowing and elaborate as an Arab robe, while many of *The Mint*'s sentences are as taut as the breeches of the Royal Air Force man. But the tight, almost

Lawrence in later life, during the time he was serving a second stint, under the surname Shaw, in the Royal Air Force. He told his friend Robert Graves that he had enlisted in the armed services because "it was the nearest modern equivalent of going into a monastery in the Middle Ages."

broken quality of Lawrence's literary voice in *The Mint* reflects the tremendous strain that the coarse, male atmosphere was putting on his defenses and on his confidence in his ability to translate the experience into something safely artistic. Instead, he worried, his book would sound like confession.

"I can't write it, because in literature such things haven't even been, and can't be," Lawrence confided in a letter to Lionel Curtis, a fellow at All Souls at Oxford, shortly after arrival at the barracks of the Royal Tank Corps:

> To record the acts of Hut 12 would produce a moral-medical case book, not a work of art but a document. It isn't the filth of it which hurts me, because you can't call filthy the pursuit of a bitch by a dog, or the mating of birds in springtime . . . but I lie in bed night after night with this catcalling carnality seething up and down the hut, fed by streams of fresh matter from twenty lecherous mouths . . . and my mind aches with the rawness of it.

The Mint was finished by 1928, and signed by "352087 A/c [Aircraftman] Ross." But even without his name on it, Lawrence had good reason to believe it was unpublishable. The picture he painted of military service was not the one the bigwigs in the air force wished to convey. "I feel all of a tremble in case it gets out and into the hands of people who do not know life as it is," wrote his friend and adviser Air Marshal Hugh Trenchard, to whom Lawrence had sent a draft. At Trenchard's request, Lawrence agreed to delay publication, though the professional relief of the air marshal was no doubt matched by the personal relief of the author. Even a "medical case book" that trembled as close to the edge of obscenity and homosexuality as *The Mint* did might have exposed its author to lawsuits and scandal. In 1898, when the famous sexologist Havelock Ellis had published accounts of homosexuality in his *Psychopathia Sexualis,* the publisher had been fined heavily. And as late as 1928, when Lawrence's publisher, Jonathan Cape, had printed Radclyffe Hall's openly lesbian novel *The Well of Loneliness,* scandal struck again. An English judge, and the public, declared the book obscene. "I would rather," said the editor of the Sunday *Times,* "give a healthy boy or a healthy girl a vial of prussic acid than this novel."

The Mint would not be published until 1955, long after its author's death. But even as Lawrence was writing it, the sharp observations of sexologists like Havelock Ellis and his psychological successor Sigmund Freud were burning more effectively than any acid through the old Victorian notions of "healthy boys and girls," corroding the structures of sexual denial, and leaving men like Lawrence painfully aware of their impulses. "Hut 12 shows me the truth behind Freud," Lawrence wrote to Lionel Curtis. "Sex is an integer in all of us, and the nearer nature we are, the more constantly, the more completely a product of that integer. These fellows are the reality, and you and I, the selves who used to meet in London and talk of fleshless things, are only the outward wrapping."

To throw himself right up against the fleshy nature of masculinity, and yet somehow try to get beyond it—that was Lawrence's real crusade. He used a number of strategies in his air force and army years—his work as a mechanic, for example, on airplanes, high-speed boats, and motorcycles. Machines met Lawrence's masculine ideals—"there are no women in machines," he told Robert Graves—because they were so reassuringly cold and sterile. His decision to enlist as a "ranker," an undifferentiated part of the military whole, was another way for him to mechanize, to become more robot than man. "Brain sleep" or "mind suicide," Lawrence called the move, and as critic Thomas O'Donnell has best noted, *The Mint* is full of descriptions that transform men into machines. Aircraftmen, for example, become "blue cylinders." One man's genitals are described as "a bicycle pump and a bag."

The machines Lawrence loved, of course, were themselves a means of transcending natural experience—they moved, and moved fast. "In speed we hurl ourselves beyond the body," Lawrence wrote of riding on his motorbike. ". . . Bones. Blood. Flesh. All pressed inward together." The sight of Lawrence racing around on his motorbike became so common for the men in the tank corps that they gave him a new nickname—Broughie Shaw. Lawrence named his bikes—Boanerges, a biblical name meaning Son of Thunder, was his favorite—and each time one broke he bought, and rechristened, another. He drove as fast as he could, ignoring crashes, as if by accelerating he could roar out of his own doubts and longings. "When my mood gets too hot . . . I pull out my motor bike and hurl it top-speed through these unfit roads for hour after hour," he wrote to Lionel Curtis. Once again, his daredevil approach appealed to the more staid members of English society—Lady Astor rode in his sidecar on more than one occasion, and George Bernard and Charlotte Shaw gave him a new motorcycle after his return from a posting in India.

When stationed in England, Lawrence's destination as he roared across the country roads was another kind of escape: a small cottage called Clouds Hill. He rented the virtually abandoned cottage from a relative (later buying it outright), and he spent many weekends and evenings fixing it up and finding peace from barracks life. "My cottage is a gem of gems—in the eyes of its owner. It is as ugly as my sins, bleak, angular, small, unstable," he wrote to Lady Astor.

Lawrence in 1935, just after his retirement from the Royal Air Force. To a friend, he described himself at the time as "gray-haired and toothless, half-blind and shaking at the knees." To another he claimed that "the active part of life is over," but he retained his enthusiasm for bicycling and riding motorcycles.

At Clouds Hill, Lawrence established his own queer kind of boy-scout world. No alcohol was allowed (guests drank water or tea), food was served out of cans, overnight guests slept in sleeping bags, and dishes were washed by piling them all in the bathtub and pouring hot water over them. Clouds Hill became a meeting place for Lawrence's two social worlds: literary figures such as E. M. Forster and Robert Graves, as well as servicemen who were invited there to relax and listen to classical music. To the recruits, Lawrence acted as don and cultural mentor, playing them records on a huge gramophone he set up in the corner. "We have just been playing your music," Lawrence wrote to the composer Edward Elgar in 1933. "Three of us, a sailor, a Tank Corps soldier, and myself . . . and we agreed that you must be written to and told . . . that this Symphony gets further under our skins than anything else in the record library at Clouds Hill."

It was in the controlled comfort of Clouds Hill that Lawrence was also able to explore the awkward pleasures of learning lessons, as well as teaching them. It was here that he built his relationship with the young, strapping soldier named John Bruce. Bruce, whose nickname was "Jock," was a 19-year-old Scotsman, the son of a dairy farmer, stationed in the same hut as Lawrence in the Royal Tank Corps. Bruce usually came to visit when Lawrence was alone—interviewed later, few of the other men in the hut knew that there was anything special about their relationship. Off and on for more than ten years, Bruce acted as Lawrence's paid taskmaster—drawing a small salary in exchange for putting his employer through a regimen of exercises, and occasionally, beatings.

Bruce explained the details of the relationship to Phillip Knightley and Colin Simpson. Lawrence never gave Bruce a direct order to beat him. Instead, Bruce received letters from a mysterious fictional relative called the "Old Man." "Lawrence said he had heard from the Old Man that he was in disgrace," Bruce remembered of one such episode. "He had failed to attend church parades and had been a disappointment in many ways." The letters gave Bruce instructions: to pick up a birch rod that had been delivered to a nearby railway station to administer the beatings, for example, and to record Lawrence's reactions during each discipline session. The afternoon after the first beating, Bruce told Knightley and Simpson, Lawrence reported that the Old Man insisted it be done again with Lawrence's trousers down. Bruce gave him twelve strokes. "Give me another one for luck," Lawrence said.

Lawrence and Bruce would continue this relationship long after Bruce had gone on to marriage and a career in engineering. Lawrence, in fact, would be godfather to Bruce's son, and every year would pay a small amount of money into a fund for the boy. Bruce, and on occasion other young men who he hired, would take part in Lawrence's disciplining. Bruce claims that he was devoted to Lawrence, but he admits that he needed the money, and it was not an easy relationship for either man. Not long after it began, Bruce was kicked out of the tank corps. According to Knightley and Simpson, when he asked for an explanation, he was told simply, "Ask the Arab."

Lawrence, never happy in the tank corps, was wracked with depression after Bruce left. The recruits there were harder and meaner than they had been in the air force, and some of them beat Lawrence so badly that they drew blood. When he complained, the recruits held a mock court-martial and ordered him to be silent. Much to his friends' alarm,

Lawrence's already tortured letters began to hint at suicide—George Bernard Shaw was concerned enough to write to Hogarth, and both Shaw and John Buchan expressed concern to Prime Minister Stanley Baldwin. Hogarth, with usual insight, acknowledged that Lawrence was choosing to suffer: "I cannot conceive of any Government post, such as the P.M. [Prime Minister] could offer, which Lawrence would accept. . . . He enlisted in order to have the padlocks riveted onto him." But in August 1925 Lawrence was allowed to return to the air force.

Lawrence's famous friends knew virtually nothing about Bruce: most were too busy thinking of his life as a private to think much about his private life. Perhaps Lawrence meant it to be that way, knowing that by doing something obviously unconventional, his even more shocking behavior would go unnoticed. A "maddening masquerade," George Bernard Shaw called Lawrence's enlistment. Forster, who felt Lawrence was punishing himself for his role in betraying the Bedouin, said that his friend was "inside a membrane of absurdity which has worn so thin that it is amazing he cannot see the light. Those damn Arabs are all right and he knows it." D. H. Lawrence, the modernist writer who shared both name and celebrity with T. E., seemed to be irritated by his contemporary: in his famous book, *Women in Love,* the female protagonist is in love with a gamekeeper she says is "like Colonel C.E. Florence, who preferred to become a private soldier again." The girl's father, no doubt speaking for the author, is unimpressed: "He saw too much advertisement behind all the humility."

The misogynistic edge to D. H. Lawrence's little joke about "Florence"—saying homosexual men are like women is one of the oldest of homophobic, heterosexual male strategies—had an echo in Lawrence's own thoughts. The truth is that Lawrence's preoccupation with men did not make him particularly kind to women. "Women? I like some women. I don't like their sex. It's as obvious as red hair," Lawrence wrote. He insisted that there were no great English women writers and told an artist friend that women's naked bodies expressed "so little." In *Seven Pillars,* Lawrence seemed delighted by the fact that "from end to end of it, there was nothing female in the Arab revolt but the camels." The rare appearances of women in Lawrence's writing—

there are hardly any—are usually accompanied by some reference to bodily unsanitariness. And yet in the years after the war, it was with a woman, Charlotte Shaw, that Lawrence achieved perhaps his deepest psychological intimacy since his time with Dahoum.

At age 65, Charlotte Shaw was old enough to be Lawrence's mother, and in some ways she treated him like one, sending him encouraging notes about *Seven Pillars* ("If you don't know it is a great book, what is the use of anyone telling you so") and hampers of food. But with Charlotte, Lawrence had the kind of communication that was impossible with his own mother. He told her about Bruce, who "comes up here quite often on Sundays, will only enter if I'm alone, and glares and glowers at me till I put some Beethoven on the gramophone." He confessed his need to write about Deraa: "I shouldn't tell you, because decent men don't talk about such things . . . to earn five minutes respite from a pain which drove me mad, I gave away the only possession we are born into the world with—our bodily integrity."

They were an odd couple—the plump, bespectacled Charlotte and the thin, intense T. E.—but they made sense together. They were both Anglo-Irish, they were both articulate and private, and they were both deeply ambivalent about their family backgrounds. T. E. told Charlotte about his illegitimacy; she told him in turn how she had disliked her mother intensely and blamed her for the death of her father. Charlotte's more-than-twenty-year-long marriage to Shaw had never been consummated, because she—and this, too, she had in common with T. E.—was repulsed by the idea of bearing children. Years later, reading these confessions, George Bernard Shaw would remark that he had never fully known his wife until reading her letters to Lawrence.

Some of the most intense correspondence between Lawrence and Charlotte Shaw occurred while he was stationed in India, where he was posted at the end of 1926. He had been sent there at his own request, wanting to be as far away from England as possible when the long-overdue subscriber's edition of *Seven Pillars* and its mass-market abridgment, *Revolt in the Desert,* were published. Charlotte took care of Clouds Hill, and Lawrence took a job at the engine repair shop in Karachi (now in Pakistan). But the imperial legacy of the city—Richard Burton had been stationed there, and it had long been a center for British intelligence agents—seemed to give Lawrence no inclination to explore its mysteries. "We stay still, and are physically taken care of, like stock cattle," Lawrence wrote to his mother, who was then working as a missionary with his eldest brother in China. Lawrence did find time to undertake, for money, a translation of *The Odyssey*. He also wrote a series of literary reviews for the *London Spectator,* signing them simply "C.D.," the initials of the last railroad station he had seen in England.

Reviews of Lawrence's own work were glowing. "Lawrence of Arabia already a Legend," proclaimed the cover of the *New York Times Book Review* when *Revolt in the Desert* was published in the United States in 1927. In England *Revolt* was a best-seller, and Winston Churchill ranked it as a classic equal to *Gulliver's Travels* and *Robinson Crusoe.* Hogarth wrote a long review in the London *Times* describing the subscriber's edition of *Seven Pillars,* which included the rape scene, the poem to "S.A.," and other personal revelations, and within days ads began to appear in the papers offering money to anyone willing to lend out the volume. Charlotte Shaw sent Lawrence a whole packet of favorable reviews, which he in turn enthusiastically summarized for Hogarth. It was one of the last letters he would write his old mentor, who died late in 1927.

The legend that Hogarth had done so much to create, however, was growing again. Not long after Lawrence was moved to a station near the Afghanistan border in 1928, rumors began to fly that he was leading an anti-Communist insurrection. It was a fiction straight out of Kipling's *Kim*—Lawrence had been seen, disguised as a Muslim holy man, rallying the Afghanis against the Russian empire. India filed a complaint with the British. A mob beat up a real holy man in Lahore. Russian and French ambassadors demanded to know what Lawrence was doing so close to the border. An anti-imperialist crowd, led by a Communist member of Parliament, burned Lawrence in effigy in London. Overwhelmed by the controversy, the air force sent him back home.

Lawrence was to climb down at Plymouth rather than London: wanting him to maintain as low a profile as possible, the air force had sent a boat to pick him up right off the ship. But the press was there anyway, with dozens of writers and cameramen in hired boats, watching and waiting. The door swung open, the rope ladder Lawrence was meant to climb down snagged, and for several minutes the small, slight figure was framed there, caught in the lenses and lights of the cameras. He looked very thin, but strong, and he bore the attention with no discernible trace of anxiety. Was Lawrence's heart bobbing like the small speedboat the air force had waiting for him, swelling and falling with the sudden burst of publicity? Had he missed the limelight, or did he dread it? What emotions did that calm face conceal as the military motorboat sped him away from the scene, the shouts of the journalists falling like raindrops into the cold, English sea?

Ironically, it was on the water that Lawrence would find his greatest peace while in the air force. From his return to England in 1929 until his retirement in 1935, he would serve as an adviser and pilot on high-speed boats, instructing other soldiers on their use and racing across the water with the same abandon he had always showed on land. He would continue to spend time at Clouds Hill, to which he would retire in 1935, occasionally fighting off or fleeing from the journalists who would throw stones on the roof in the hopes of making him come out. Toward the end of his military service he had a card made up—"To tell you in the future that I shall be writing very few letters," it read—but often, in sending it to his friends, he ended up enclosing long letters as well. "If you meet (Prime Minister) Baldwin in the near future," he wrote to John Buchan just before his retirement, "will you please tell him that the return to the air force secured me by him (on your initiation) has given me the only really contented years of my life? Please say that I've worked (and played) all the time like a trooper: that my spell of service has been spent in doing my best to raise the pride and respect of the ranks, and to make them pleased with their duties."

Lawrence's younger brother, A. W. Lawrence, would come often to Clouds Hill to help him with the gardening and the fixing up. Lawrence's friends—servicemen and visitors from London—were his other family. Occasionally he would travel to visit Bruce for a dose of discipline, though the anguish of the early days of that relationship was nowhere evident. With John Buchan, the Shaws, Lady Astor, and Winston Churchill, he maintained happy relations. If, as World War II and another conflict with Germany approached, he had any particular interest in politics, there was no sign of it. When Lady Astor invited him to discuss the reorganization of the government with some powerful politicians, he refused. When a journalist asked if he was going to make himself "Dictator of England," he dismissed the idea outright. Another friend, Henry Williamson, wanted to put him in touch with Adolf Hitler, Nazi Germany's dictator, but Lawrence seemed more intent on listening to his gramophone than to the call to arms. He did invite Williamson to lunch, jumping on his motorbike and going to the nearby army camp of Bovington to wire an invitation.

On the way back from the post office, roaring as always down one hill and up another, Lawrence suddenly saw two boys on bicycles in front of him. He swerved to avoid them, and crashed. Six days later, after having fallen into a coma in the Bovington hospital, the greatest hero of World War I was dead. "Too Big for Wealth and Glory," the banner headline of the *Daily Sketch* newspaper announced on May 19, 1935. "Lawrence the Soldier Dies To Live for Ever." Rumors about Lawrence's death were soon spreading like wildfire: he had been killed by fascists desperate to learn the secrets of England's air defense! He had killed himself, knowing that his scandalous sexual relations with enlisted men were about to be revealed! He was actually alive, and had been sighted leading a rebellion in southern Sudan! Whether as Lawrence or Shaw, officer or private, he never stopped commanding the imagination.

As he wished, Lawrence had no military parade or elaborate burial ceremony to mark his death. But at Moreton Church, just across the fields from Clouds Hill, there had never been such a glamorous and glittering assortment of people as those who turned out to watch his plain, unmarked coffin being lowered in the earth. The Shaws were away, but Winston Churchill, Lady Astor, and Lionel Curtis all attended. Members of the Royal Tank Corps and Royal Air Force were there to carry the coffin. Colonel Newcombe, who had walked through the Sinai with Lawrence and Dahoum, was a pallbearer, too. So was Sir

Acolytes, clergymen, pallbearers, and mourners leave the village church of Moreton on the afternoon of May 21, 1935, following Lawrence's funeral.

Ronald Storrs, who had invited Lawrence along on that first trip to Arabia and now carried him to a very different destination.

Earlier, with the permission of the family, Storrs had entered the church to take a picture of Lawrence lying in his coffin. It was hard for him to focus as he stared through the lens at his friend, head swathed in white bandages, but it is easy to imagine what he saw: a fair-haired Arab leader, lying at peace in the white silk robes of a Meccan prince. It is a picture that the artist Eric Kennington carved into stone, making a full-length statue of Lawrence reclining in Arab robes, with his hand on a curved dagger and his head on a camel saddle. That statue lies in the Church of St. Martin, in Wareham, and even now, a young boy, dreamy and determined, may be bicycling to visit it. It is a monument to fantasy, made in the style reserved for England's greatest crusader kings.

CHAPTER TWELVE

TOWARD A GAY LAWRENCE

"Most wars were to be a war of contact. Ours was to be a war of detachment," Lawrence wrote about the battles he waged against the Turks. His statement, the heart of his guerrilla war philosophy, could almost have been the motto for generations of men who sat, in very different circumstances, in English drawing rooms halfway across the globe. The war of detachment—the ability to appear unconcerned with the desires and demands of society—had long been a familiar conflict for men who loved men. The "frivolous" clothing worn by the dandy; the aesthete's practiced concern for art objects rather than family; the biting wittiness of homosexuals who, forbidden from speaking frankly about their own desires, choose instead to mock frankness and desire as a whole—all of these are weapons of detachment, still deployed by gay men to contain the hostile forces that outnumber and surround them.

"If you knew all about me," Lawrence wrote E. M. Forster in 1927, "you'd think very little of me." But friends rarely agreed with Lawrence's harsh self-assessments. "I consider him the most marvelous human being I ever met," Florence Hardy said about him in a letter to Robert Graves. "It is not his exploits in Arabia that attract me, nor the fact that he is a celebrity: it is his character that is so splendid."

"But Nature is so uncomfortable. Grass is hard and lumpy and damp and full of dreadful insects. Why, even Morris' poorest workman can make you a more comfortable seat than the whole of nature can," Oscar Wilde wrote in his essay *The Decay of Lying*. More than a century later, his words ring out like an anthem for gay men and lesbians tired of being told that their behavior is unnatural, that men and men or women and women are not "made" to go together. For Wilde and other homosexuals in the generation before Lawrence, art and artifice offered an escape hatch from the relentless, oppressive discussion of the natural. "The first duty in life is to be as artificial as possible," Wilde observed. Other authors, like Joris-Karl Huysman, spelled out some suggestions on how that duty might be met, cataloging super-refined pleasures like perfume sniffing and the wearing of white velvet suits in his 1884 bible of decadence called, appropriately, *Against Nature*.

And Lawrence, though far from the perfumes of Huysman or the lilies of Wilde, was against nature too. He loved the desert because there he was outside, away from the messiness, the discomfort of a system that expected him to produce something—heterosexuality, a child, a successful career—he never felt he could deliver. The English countryside is "obese," he wrote home as a twenty-six-year-old from Syria. The desert of *Seven Pillars,* on the other hand, he found spare and clean, just "the heaven above and the unspotted earth beneath."

Lawrence was not the first, or the last, to feel that cleansing relief. Many Western women and men, heterosexual and homosexual, have been able to rest easier in the East. Isabelle Eberhardt, an illegitimate daughter of European aristocrats who traveled through Algeria dressed as an Arab cavalryman in the early 1900s; Jean Genet, the brilliant gay writer and ex-convict who went to fight alongside the Palestinians in Lebanon in 1970; Paul Bowles and William Burroughs and Allen Ginsberg, Americans whose writing captured the lives and lusts of gay foreigners and the Moroccan men they slept with—these are only a few of the individuals who were drawn to the heat and light of Middle Eastern countries, far from the natural place for them to make a home and family.

And even when in England, Lawrence challenged the idea of the natural. His love of machines was one way of doing that; his constant thwarting of expectations about usefulness and productivity was another. Lawrence was a plainer man than Wilde, but it is not so far from Wilde's famous witticism—"It is so hard living up to one's blue china"—to the Greek inscription Lawrence carved himself over the doorway of Clouds Hill: "I don't care."

Friends and biographers of Lawrence, of course, do care about what lay behind his detachment, or more specifically, care to erase the fact that homosexuality had anything to do with it. When allegations about Lawrence's sexuality began to surface, Lowell Thomas rushed to the defense, stating that anyone who has been in lengthy contact with "pathologues" knows that they will give away their secret eventually. He himself had met all types of "them," Thomas noted, and his father was a doctor. Lawrence's companion at Carchemish, Leonard Woolley, who wrote in great detail about his friend's relationship with Dahoum, went on to insist that Lawrence was "in no sense a pervert" and had "a remarkably clean mind."

Lawrence's writings, as well as his person, have been defended against the claim of homosexuality, but even the brightest young Oxonian would have a hard time following the mental gymnastics of those determined to prove that the poem to "S.A." was written for someone other than Salim Ahmed, whose nickname was Dahoum. Robert Graves suggests that S.A. was short for "Son Altesse," a poetic French term of address, meaning "His or Her Highness," that Lawrence might have used for Farida El-Akle, his female Arabic teacher in Syria. Knightley and Simpson report that Dr. Ernest El-Tunyan, a friend of Lawrence's, thought the initials stood for Sarah Aaronsohn, a Zionist spy who worked for the British in Palestine (and whom Lawrence met just once, if at all). Farida El-Akle said she thought the "S.A" stood for "Syria-Arabia." Lawrence himself once suggested that "S.A" was meant to be a person of neutral gender. That ambiguity will sound familiar to any of us who have ever changed the way we speak to conceal a secret bond with someone of the same sex. "What time are you meeting your friend?" someone will ask. "I'm meeting *them* at 2:00," comes the studiedly casual reply.

With the same vigor that Lawrence described his own and other's homosexual experiences in *Seven Pillars,* others have repressed them. His brother Arnold said that Lawrence died a virgin, as if his interactions with the bey at Deraa and with Bruce at Clouds Hill did not count. Jeremy Wilson, the "authorized" biographer of Lawrence, refers to Farraj and Daud as lifelong friends, when Lawrence tells us they were lovers. The Wilson biography is one of many that tells us something that Lawrence did not—that as a young man, Lawrence had proposed marriage to a young neighbor named Janet Laurie. Less often repeated is the fact that when Lawrence first saw her, in church, she was dressed like a boy.

Church and religious faith are often invoked to explain away Lawrence's sexuality. His "subjection of the body was achieved by methods advocated by the saints whose lives he had read," his brother wrote in 1937, though we know that Lawrence never really turned to God or the saints for guidance. Lawrence's faith was in hard, tough men. *Seven Pillars* and *The Mint* are full of nothing else.

Other biographies—like Knightley and Simpson's, and John Mack's—have presented much more complicated views of Lawrence's sexuality, but debate still rages. "I do not believe there is a shred of proven evidence that he was gay," one outraged academic wrote to the editor of this book. "I find it rather disheartening that a series such as this would include him without proof documented in some way." If by "proof documented" one means a picture of Lawrence in the bedroom or a clear statement of his "homosexuality," there of course will be none, since neither indoor instamatics nor the idea of a defined homosexual identity were popular in his day. It was dangerous to even write explicitly about homosexuality without labeling yourself a criminal—even "convicted" homosexual Oscar Wilde did not have his most explicit discussion of male-male love, *De Profundis,* published while he lived. E. M. Forster's homosexual novel, *Maurice,* would not be printed until 1971. Instead, Lawrence left us the facts of his life: his love for Dahoum in particular and for men in general, the fact that he never married or expressed any interest in doing so after returning from the Middle East, the sexual warmth that swelled through him while the Turks "played unspeakably" with him at Deraa, his confession to Robert Graves that he had enjoyed being "buggered," and his relationship with Bruce. Some will say that what Lawrence did with Bruce wasn't homosexuality, or even sexuality at all. But why not? Can anyone believe that to Lawrence either the sex of the person beating him or the fact of his orgasm was unimportant? Or is sex only defined when genital meets genital, or as a process that involves pleasure but no pain? Certainly many people, heterosexual and homosexual, would be surprised to hear it.

A better question to ask seems to be why it is so important for heterosexuals to wrench Lawrence from the homosexual category. Gay men have, in our own way and in our own private language, done our best to keep him in, passing Lawrence and his work like a specially minted coin from one friend to another. When Christopher Isherwood, the young homosexual writer, met the slightly older E. M. Forster, *Seven Pillars* was the first thing they talked about (Forster lent Isherwood his copy). Isherwood, with his homosexual friend W. H. Auden, wrote a play based on Lawrence, *The Ascent of F-6,* about a military hero who is both a scholar and a man of action. Auden, a brilliant poet, wrote a sonnet based on Lawrence, too, about a public figure:

> Who, say astonished critics, lived at home;
> Did little jobs about the house with skill
> And nothing else; could whistle; would sit still
> Or potter round the garden; answered some
> Of his long marvelous letters but kept none.

Critics will charge that Lawrence's homosexuality is pure fantasy. So what? Fantasy is a part of everything that Lawrence means to history. The war in the Middle East, by Lawrence's own account, was a "sideshow of a sideshow," of little strategic importance when compared to the great battles of Europe or the revolution in Russia that were occurring simultaneously. Yet Lawrence's work has fascinated for so long precisely because we can dream of it, in Lawrence's words, "with open eyes." It is a dream, not a reality, that allowed biographer after biographer to describe Lawrence as the uncrowned king of the Arabs, when we know no Arabs ever mistook his blue-eyed, clean-shaven face for one of their own. It is a dream, not a reality, that led people to see Lawrence in the guise of an Afghani holy man, or a rebel leader in southern Sudan. It is a dream that has moved more than 50 authors to write biographies of Lawrence, in English, French, German, Japanese, Arabic, and other languages. By any scientific standard, if we demanded a "shred of proven evidence," Lawrence might not be considered a hero at all.

So imagine what you will. I do, thinking of Lawrence's final moments, as he raced down that hill on his big black motorcycle only to see two startled delivery boys on bicycles. Had Lawrence been daydreaming of another May, the one he spent riding to Aqaba? Could he have glanced up to see the faces of two Arab boys, the beautiful young lovers, Farraj and Daud? And did he know it was an English nurse that changed the dressings on his wounds in the hospital? Or did Lawrence feel the gentle hand of Dahoum, wiping down his feverish brow, and leading him once more toward the ruined clay house where, together, the two could breathe in the empty, desert wind that for Lawrence had always been the cleanest, purest, and most sustaining air of all?

FURTHER READING

Aldington, Richard. *Lawrence of Arabia: A Biographical Enquiry*. Chicago: Henry Regnery, 1955.

Brown, Malcolm, and Julia Cave. *A Touch of Genius: The Life of T. E. Lawrence*. New York: Paragon House, 1989.

Graves, Robert. *Lawrence and the Arabs*. London: Butler & Tanner Ltd., 1927.

James, Lawrence. *The Golden Warrior: The Life and Legend of Lawrence of Arabia*. New York: Paragon House, 1993.

Knightley, Phillip, and Colin Simpson. *The Secret Lives of Lawrence of Arabia*. New York: McGraw Hill, 1970.

Lawrence, T. E. *The Letters of T. E. Lawrence*. Edited by David Garnett. New York: Doubleday, Doran, 1938.

———. *The Mint*. 1955. Reprint. New York: Norton & Co., 1963.

———. *Secret Despatches from Arabia*. Edited by A. W. Lawrence. N.p.: 1939.

———. *Seven Pillars of Wisdom*. 1926. Reprint. New York: Penguin Books, 1976.

Mack, John. *A Prince of Our Disorder: The Life of T. E. Lawrence*. Boston: Little, Brown and Company, 1976.

Mousa, Suleiman. *T. E. Lawrence: An Arab View*. Translated by A. Butros. London: Oxford University Press, 1967.

Tabachnik, Stephen E., and Christopher Matheson. *Images of Lawrence*. London: Jonathan Cape Limited, 1988.

Thomas, Lowell. *With Lawrence in Arabia*. 1924. Reprint. New York: Popular Library, 1961.

Wilson, Jeremy. *Lawrence of Arabia: The Authorized Biography of T. E. Lawrence*. New York: Macmillan, 1992.

CHRONOLOGY

1888	Born Thomas Edward Lawrence on August 15, in Tremadoc, Wales
1907	Begins studying at Jesus College, Oxford University
1909	Journeys to Middle East for the first time; returns in 1910 on archaeological expedition and stays for four years
1914	Maps Sinai Peninsula during his first espionage-related mission; World War I breaks out; assigned to Cairo intelligence office
1916	Arab rebellion against Turkish rule begins; British and French sign secret Sykes-Picot Agreement
1917	Lawrence travels through the desert enlisting help from local tribes to capture Aqaba; receives promotion to major and a medal from the king; begins leading raids and planting explosives; journeys to Deraa, where he is allegedly raped
1918	Offers his resignation but is convinced to stay on in Middle East; awarded medal for bravery; plays important role in series of battles culminating in Turkish retreat from Damascus
1919	Attends Paris Peace Conference with Arab leader Feisal; arranges meeting between Feisal and Zionist leaders, sparking first Arab-Jewish peace agreement; British and French divide Middle East between themselves; Lawrence accepts fellowship at All Souls College at Oxford to write a book
1921	Joins Churchill's Colonial Office to forge new settlement in Middle East
1922	Enlists as Private T. E. Ross in the air force

1923	Joins Royal Tank Corps as Private Shaw
1925	Rejoins Royal Air Force
1926	Stationed in India; *Seven Pillars of Wisdom* published in England
1929	Returns to England after rumors of his involvement in an anti-Communist insurrection near the Afghanistan border
1935	Retires from military service; dies in motorbike crash

INDEX

Daniel Wolfe is a New York City writer who worked with former First Lady of Egypt Jehan el-Sadat and Pakistani prime minister Benazir Bhutto on their autobiographies. Mr. Wolfe's work has also appeared in the *Guardian* and the *New York Times Book Review*.

Martin Duberman is Distinguished Professor of History at the Graduate Center for the City University of New York and the founder and director of the Center for Gay and Lesbian Studies. One of the country's foremost historians, he is the author of 15 books and numerous articles and essays. He has won the Bancroft Prize for *Charles Francis Adams* (1960); two Lambda awards for *Hidden from History: Reclaiming the Gay and Lesbian Past,* an anthology that he coedited; and a special award from the National Academy of Arts and Letters for his overall "contributions to literature." His play *In White America* won the Vernon Rice/Drama Desk Award in 1964. His other works include *James Russell Lowell* (1966), *Black Mountain: An Exploration in Community* (1972), *Paul Robeson* (1989), *Cures: A Gay Man's Odyssey* (1991), and *Stonewall* (1993).

Professor Duberman received his Ph.D. in history from Harvard University in 1957 and served as professor of history at Yale University and Princeton University from 1957 until 1972, when he assumed his present position at the City University of New York.

PICTURE CREDITS:

Archive Photos: pp. 2, 72, 86, 93, 101, 103, 129; Ashmolean Museum: pp. 23, 36; The Bettmann Archive: pp. 71, 110; Bodleian Library: pp. 20, 28, 124; British Film Institute/Stills, Posters and Design: p. 64; The British Library: p. 49; Culver Pictures: p. 96; The Hulton Deutsch Collection: pp. 88, 130, 136, 142; The Imperial War Museum: pp. 14, 42, 44, 52, 57, 60, 67, 68, 76, 81, 83, 106, 119; Liddell Hart Centre for Military Archives: pp. 78, 114–15; Magdalen College: p. 25; Merton College: p. 39; Oxfordshire County Council Library Services: p. 32; The Tank Museum: p. 108; UPI/Bettmann: p. 139.

Map (p. 17) by Gary Tong.